THE PHONEBOOK

THE PHONE BOOK

BREAKTHROUGH
NEUROLINGUISTIC
PHONE SKILLS
FOR PROFIT AND
ENLIGHTENMENT

RICHARD A. ZARRO
& PETER BLUM

Metamorphous Press
Portland, OR 97210

The excerpt on pg. 29 from "Phone Calls From The Fast Lane: Life Inside a Freeway Telephone Booth," by Robert Reinhold, August 20, 1987, is quoted from *The New York Times.* © 1987 by The New York Times Company. Reprinted by permission.

The excerpt on pg. 30 from *In Search of Excellence*, by Thomas J. Peters and Robert H. Waterman, Jr., © 1982, is reprinted by permission of Harper and Row.

The excerpt on pp. 43-44 from *Sound Medicine* by Laeh Maggie Garfield, © 1987 is reprinted by permission of Celestial Arts.

Published by

Metamorphous Press
P.O. Box 10616
Portland, OR 97210

Copyright © 1989 by Richard A. Zarro and Peter Blum
Editorial and Art Direction by Lori Stephens
Printed in the United States of America

Zarro, Richard A.
The phone book : breakthrough neurolinguistic phone skills for profit and enlightenment / [Richard A. Zarro, Peter Blum].
p. cm.
ISBN 1-55552-011-1 (pbk.) : $10.95
1. Telephone in business. 2. Telephone etiquette. I. Blum, Peter, 1947- . II. Title.
HF5541.T4Z37   1993
651.7'3--dc20   92-45703

DEDICATION

To the staff and volunteers at Family of Woodstock, the oldest continuously operating telephone hotline in the U.S., and the real Hotline of this story. Their training and the time I have spent on shift have been invaluable in adding to my own phone skills. - P.B.

To Dr. Ronald Zarro, the telephone master who uses the phone like a Stradivarius violin and taught me that God has an 800 number. To my parents, Eugene and Vita, who supported my views even when they were controversial and who embodied the very best of communication skills especially over the telephone. And to my teenage daughter, Hope, who showed me that life can be conducted over the telephone with great ease and grace. - R.A.Z.

ACKNOWLEDGEMENTS

This book was made possible with the help of a number of people. The authors would like to gratefully acknowledge the teachings of Richard Bandler and John Grinder, founders of Neuro-Linguistic Programming. Thanks to Steve Chun for quick and efficient copyediting, to Rob Berman for meticulous proofreading, and to Tony Klück for his magical illustrations.

In addition, we are grateful for the feedback and support along the way of Amy Blum, Henry Blum, Merrily Blum, Martha Frankel, Mikhail Horowitz, Jill Kavner, Cathy Lewis, Carol MacDonald, Michael Perkins, Sue Pilla, George and Susan Quasha, Scott Siegal, Andrea Stern, Lama Tharchin, Artie Traum, Bardor Tulku Rinpoche, Joan Walker, and Marilyn Wright.

CONTENTS

Introduction   9

Chapter One
Even E.T. Had to Phone Home:
Restoring the Awe and Wonder of the Phone Call   11

Chapter Two
In Which I Discover The Three Types of Phoners   32

Chapter Three
Pretending To Be Natural, or
How I Got to Be a True Phoney   61

Chapter Four
How To Be Cool With A Hot Phone   70

Chapter Five
Phones Have Feelings Too!
Befriending The Phone   84

Chapter Six
The Hyp Phonist   117

Epilogue
May the Circuits Be Unbroken   146

INTRODUCTION

You are about to take a magical journey. This is a story about the awakening of a sleeping prince, and his discovery of an amazing invention that puts the whole world in his hands. It is as much a journey of *rediscovery* as discovery.

The telephone has been taken for granted. The extraordinary has become ordinary. We hope that by the time you finish this book you will look at the phone with new eyes, hear it as if for the first time, and feel the power of mastering new communication skills. Have fun.

CHAPTER ONE

EVEN E.T. HAD TO PHONE HOME

Restoring the Awe and Wonder of the Phone

"**A**re you okay?"

As I opened my eyes, I saw an older man's friendly face hovering over me. What a frightening dream that had been!

My shirt was soaked with sweat, and a corner of my flight pillow was jammed in my mouth. I looked down and saw that my right hand was clasped tightly over my left wrist, where my watch alarm had accidentally gone off. I was more than a bit embarrassed.

"I'm sorry, I was dreaming. I hope I didn't disturb you or any of the other passengers." I sat up in my seat and glanced around the first class compartment of the jumbo jet.

"Not at all, I don't think anybody else heard you."

Up to that point I hadn't really paid much attention to the man sitting next to me. I had been too caught up in my own problems and exhaustion. He looked like a normal, tired businessman, sort of an older version of myself.

"I must admit, I was curious. You were making some strange sounds."

I leaned back in my chair and tried to decide how much to tell this guy. Out of the corner of my eye I gave him the once-over. He was wearing a beautiful tailored suit, a gold watch worth more than my car, and a ring shining like a small star on his finger. He was still turned slightly toward me and his blue eyes expressed such an open, friendly quality, that I impulsively stuck out my hand.

"Let me introduce myself. My name is Bob O'Ryan."

He gripped it, patting it with the other hand, saying "I'm glad to meet you, I'm John Deltone. My friends call me JD." Then, almost as an afterthought, he said, "Must have been some dream, your hand is all sweaty."

"I... well, you may think this is silly." I paused for a second, gathering my thoughts before going on. "But I was having a nightmare about a telephone. It was ringing and ringing and I couldn't get to it. It was really frightening."

JD was smiling again. "So that's what was going on. Your wrist alarm was going off, and you reached out and grabbed it as if your life depended on it. But you still didn't wake up when you shut it off. I don't understand what's so frightening about the phone ringing."

"Well, I'm not really sure. For the last several months it has been a recurrent nightmare. I wake up in a sweat, shaking all over and what's even worse, when I have to use the phone later in the day, I begin to get just as nervous and afraid."

"Of what, exactly?"

"Did you ever have a dream where you needed to run away and couldn't move?"

"Sure."

"Well, in my dream the person on the other end keeps saying 'Are you there?' And I try and speak and nothing comes out. I can't explain why, but it's a gut-wrenching feeling."

"It's a shame the telephone affects you that way." JD sat back in his seat as if lost in reverie. I began to drift off myself, thinking about the past two days. I had just completed my company's annual motivational seminar in California. It had been the usual whirlwind of luncheons, statistics, speakers, more statistics, and policy change meetings. I didn't feel motivated, and I didn't feel like I had learned anything that would help me.

I missed my wife Sheryl, and my two children. If I didn't have such an aversion to using the telephone I would have called them from the West Coast before my flight.

It seemed the only good thing about my trip was getting to travel in the First Class section on the flight back to New York. The airline had overbooked the business coach section and they bumped me up to First Class where there was a last-minute cancellation.

This bit of "luck" was the beginning of a remarkable chain of events. I never would have suspected that solving my problems *with the phone* would change my life so dramatically. I am now more prosperous— materially and spiritually— and more content, enjoying not only financial security, but a kind of deep relaxation that brings peace of mind.

* * *

"Really, the phone is magic," JD's voice startled me. "I give seminars on telecommunications and satellite interfaces. In my business I come in contact with lots of

"The phone is magic."

people who have to use the phone day in and day out. And you know," he said with a smile, "many of them used to have the same *hang-ups* as you do about the phone."

JD looked closely at me. "But maybe you don't want to hear all this now. I sense you have other things on your mind, Bob."

"You seem to think the phone is magic. I am tired, but I'm also curious. Do you have some advice or secrets you'd like to share about using the phone?"

"I don't know about secrets," JD laughed and glanced out the window at the ground far below. "Well, perhaps I do have *a few* secrets." He turned toward me, and his voice became passionate.

"Not very long ago the Earth was a vast mystery. All that people really knew firsthand was their immediate territory and close neighbors. Only great explorers traveled beyond the known limits of their village or valley. Only the bravest of warriors wandered out to face and chart the unknown. Very few could even conceive of the enormity of the world out there," he said pointing out the window.

"Quite something, isn't it?" JD asked." Here we are, travelling from one end of the continent to the other overnight." It *was* pretty amazing, when I stopped to think about it.

"Even as recently as 150 years ago, the inhabitants still couldn't talk to each other over long distances, beyond rudimentary means like smoke signals and drums. It was not easy to communicate. In fact, it was sometimes impossible. Then something earth-shaking happened which changed all of that, forever."

"The telephone, right?"

"Right. But *you* take it for granted. That's an attitude. The phone is fabulous! Its invention gradually allowed the construction of a communication network all over this planet. The big, unknowable world shrank radically. One simple device changed life as we knew it, not only for the most ordinary forms of communicating, but more recently, computer information and link-ups, and sending of facsimiles. Even videophone hook-ups."

"Videophones," I interrupted, "would be perfect for me. You see, I'd rather talk to a person face-to-face than over the telephone. I guess I gauge people's reactions to what I'm saying by the look on their face. It helps me figure out if I'm reaching them or not. You know, whether I should continue in that direction or choose another. You can't 'hear' someone smile on the phone."

"Sure you can!" JD said, enthusiastically.

I let that remark go, for the time being, and continued talking. "It's impersonal, especially calling somebody I haven't met—you know, the famous Cold Call! There I am, I don't even know what they look like, so I'm trying to imagine that, and worried about whether I'm interrupting them. But the worst part is, in my line of work, I have to try to act like we already have a close relationship, which is really..."

"Phone-y?" JD interjected.

"Yes, that's exactly right," I responded excitedly.

"Bob, let me repeat, you are not alone in your fear of the phone. There are a lot of people with *phonephobias*. It doesn't seem to matter if they are highly educated or not, or what their occupation is; they find the phone to be intimidating.

"Such people feel the phone is a difficult instrument to master. If you are looking for secrets, the first place I'd look at is how to change this kind of attitude."

JD's next question caught me by surprise. "Do you have any kids?"

"Yes, I've got an eight-year-old daughter, and a five-year-old boy."

"Okay. Do you remember when they were around two or three? Everytime the phone rang, they wanted to answer it, right?"

"Yup."

"Why? Because it's *fun!* A child hasn't taken the miracles around us for granted. For them it is fascinating that Grandma or Grandpa could be *in the phone.* How can you, Bob, rediscover the attitude of awe, of child-like wonder at the magic of the telephone?"

JD spotted the flight attendant walking past us in the aisle. "Excuse me, I just remembered that I have a couple of calls to make. They won't take long, and then we can talk some more, if you want. Okay?"

He waved to the flight attendant. "Barbara, hi. Can I have the in-flight phone, please."

"Certainly, sir." She walked toward the rear of the plane to get the portable phone.

"Boy, JD, you really are comfortable with the phone. Calling people from mid-air..."

"Bob, you still don't get it. It's not a chore for me, it's a joy. Communication over the phone–and I mean skillful communication–is an art form. It has its master artists. We all recognize it when we are talking to one of them on the phone. It makes us feel high, elated, and uniquely comforted. We know when we've had an extraordinary experience on the phone."

Barbara reappeared with a cordless phone. JD cradled it in his lap while he inserted his credit card and dialed a number. At that range, I guess he wasn't worried about privacy.

"Hello, Kevin? JD here. I had a fabulous time. I just wanted to thank you for the opportunity to address your company, and tell you what a wonderful employee Mary is."

He listened for a moment. "Capable? She's not only capable, she's a mind reader. Mary took care of things before I could ask her. If it weren't for her I wouldn't have felt nearly as relaxed. She's an entire support team. I'll be sending you a letter of commendation for her that I would like you to personally see goes in her file. She is really special." He stopped and listened again.

"Yes, I'd love to work with your other division. Let me check those dates." He pulled a small date book out of his attache case and flipped through it while he spoke. "I think that weekend is okay. I'll be in touch with you as soon as I get into my office to confirm. Okay, Kevin, and thanks. Take care of yourself and give your beautiful wife Susan a big kiss for me."

JD hung up, took a deep breath and let it out before dialing again. "Hello dear, it's me. Yes, the flight is on schedule. Everything's fine. I just called to say how much I love you and the kids and that I'll be arriving at Kennedy as planned. Can't wait to see you."

* * *

After JD had returned the phone to Barbara, we both ordered dinner— lobster and champagne. God, there is nothing else quite like First Class treatment. Why does it seem to take so long to treat ourselves and others like we're First Class?

"See," said JD, "there's an example of something I wanted to do spontaneously, and the phone made it possible."

"Well, you could have waited till you got back in your office on Monday to write a letter, right?"

"Sure, but there's nothing like the telephone. And there is nothing like the moment. The telephone is perfect for that kind of communication... cuts down tremendously on turn-around. You know," he said with a grin, "even E.T. had to call home!

"I even got an unexpected reward for acting on impulse. I called to compliment my assistant at the seminar, and ended up getting a $10,000 offer for another seminar. I didn't call for that reason, but that was one of the results. Ten thousand dollars for three days! Not bad, eh?"

"Not bad at all," I answered. He seemed like such a genuinely nice guy I found it hard to be jealous, but not impossible.

As the stewardess served us, JD continued to sell me on the magic of the phone.

"Now, you said earlier that you found the phone cold and impersonal, right?"

"Right!"

"Recent articles have shown that people are more effective in dealing with others, presenting their case, or even settling differences on the phone than in face-to-face communication. Over the phone, attitudes are more easily changed and concessions made."

"I find that hard to believe. Is there real research to back this up?"

"Certainly, Bob. You can call me at my office and I'll send you reprints of the articles reporting these studies."

"This is fascinating. Tell me more!"

JD took a few more bites of his food, looked out the window at the sea of white clouds and said, "For one thing, you may be overlooking one of the most unusual aspects of communicating by phone. The phone is as close as you can get to a person without them feeling uncomfortable and pulling away."

As the stewardess poured more champagne, I puzzled over JD's remark and asked him just what he meant. He turned slightly in his seat to answer, and I was aware of the extra room in First Class, and how much more comfortable I felt. In coach, if my seatmate had turned that much, we would have been playing footsie!

"Do you know what some research psychologists have said about love and space?"

"No," I answered, intrigued by the question.

"Go up to our flight attendant Barabara and strike up a conversation. And as you are doing that see how close you can get to her face."

"Why?"

"Just try it. Trust me! You're in for a phonetastic surprise "

I figured I had nothing to lose. Besides, I was really beginning to trust and like this guy, despite his bad puns. He was a storehouse of information.

I walked back to the galley area and began to chat with Barbara about the arrival time, weather, etc. During various parts of the conversation I tried, as JD had suggested, to move my face toward hers. Whenever I reached a certain point, she stepped back. If I moved my body to make up the difference, she moved further back.

After a couple of minutes, I excused myself and went back to my seat.

"So how did it go?"

"The only thing I noticed was she moved away when I leaned my face towards hers, or took a step closer."

"That's not because you have bad breath..."

He laughed and said, "I'm only kidding. Let me tell you an interesting fact. Research indicates that if you let

"The phone is as close as I can get to a person without them feeling uncomfortable and pulling away."

someone within four inches of your face, you love them. If you were one of Barbara's loved ones—parents, boyfriend, husband, or child—she wouldn't have moved away every time you moved forward. Her body language let you know how much rapport she had with you."

I had a sudden insight as to why I liked the extra few inches between seats in First Class. "Fascinating," I commented.

"Isn't it? So now let me ask you, when someone calls you on the telephone, how close are they to your face?"

"They are right next to my ear and an inch from my mouth."

"Right! And you call that distant? Impersonal? Cold?"

"Well, I never thought of it that way before..."

"There really is no other way you can get so close to a person so quickly except through using the telephone. *And everyone uses the telephone.* Everyone communicates, even when they are not saying anything. And words, Bob, are MAGIC. Communicating effectively is POWER. And since you have to do it anyway, every day, you might as well become *phonomenal*!"

All of a sudden JD's rap started to sound very familiar. I could hear my father, who had been a salesman all his life, telling me and my brother, "you are *always* selling yourself." According to Pop, all of life, personal and business, is sales, and words are the key to selling.

I could see him vividly, standing in the kitchen and addressing us as teenagers. Enthusiastically waving his finger in the air, he would say, "The power of words—dynamic communication—can change the world, galvanize nations, save marriages, and is the lifeblood of love. It can change your whole life, whether you are a businessman, a wife, a lover, a father, a son, an astronaut, a pilot, a waiter or a writer."

Going through life thinking I always had to sell myself was not my idea of a good time. I always felt people should accept me for who I am. Selling myself or my ideas seemed all hustle, little poetry. Over time, sales and communication became synonymous with Saturday chores. I vowed never to become a salesman. Never!

So much for that! After a B.A. in English and three unpublished plays, I got to the point of being forced to make a living to support my family. Despite my vow I began selling; first real estate, then insurance. At the time of that memorable flight I wasn't very happy about it. Not only did I feel like I had sold out, but I wasn't even doing that well, financially.

My sales manager said it was because I had such an abhorrence of making cold calls on the phone and getting the appointments that were necessary for any real success in the field. I knew he was right. Even though I forced myself to make my quota of calls every week, I was highly ineffective. It was a vicious cycle. The more I forced myself to use the phone, the less successful I was.

I had begun to realize I needed some new business skills, especially in communication, or I would never achieve any level of success. Even more disturbing was the realization that my father had been right all along. And here was JD, giving me a souped-up version of the same message I had not been able to hear 20 years earlier. I had the feeling that someone up there was laughing.

Coming back to the present, I noticed JD smiling as he watched me. "Dreaming again?"

"What? Oh, yeah, I guess I was daydreaming. You know, I'd love to believe what you say about the phone being magic and the power to use words. But I can't help the way I feel."

"What line of work are you in, Bob?"

"I sell insurance."

"Why did you become an insurance salesman?"

"Well, I used to be in real estate. To tell you the truth, one of the main reasons I switched was real estate required being on the phone a lot. I thought insurance would be more of a face-to-face business, but I was wrong."

"Have you ever noticed, in your family or work environment, there are people who seem to be able to play the telephone as if it were a musical instrument?"

"I'm not sure I know what you mean."

"Let me tell you a story. I once worked in an office with someone named Joan. There were about half a dozen people answering the phones and taking orders. I began to notice that more and more customers, after having placed their first order with Joan, asked for her when they called to reorder. Why was that? All of the telemarketers were courteous and efficient. All of them would process an order with the same speed.

"I began to listen to Joan when she was on the phone. She not only took the customers' orders, she was able, within a few short sentences, to establish a deep rapport with them. It was beyond just a friendly attitude. She seemed able to know just the right remark, the right tone of voice, to make them feel like they had reached a friend... someone who was interested in who *they* were, how *they* were feeling. She often joked with them about business, or their family. The extra minute resulted in extra dollars for the business. And also, Joan was having a ball."

"I know someone like that in my office."

"Good. One day I was sitting next to Joan at lunch. I asked her what her secret was. She answered, 'listening!'"

"But everybody listens..." I said.

"'I mean *really* listening. I love it,' she replied. 'I am always amazed that people are so friendly, so eager to talk to you when they know you're really interested in what they're saying.'

"Don't you ever get bored?" I asked.

"'Oh, no,' she said. 'Each time the phone rings, there's a sense of adventure, of looking forward to hearing something I've never heard, of meeting new people, listening to their stories. Everyone's life is so different and interesting.'

"Now Bob, I don't want you to get the wrong idea. Joan was not trained as a super-salesperson. The fact that she was generating more business for our company was, for her, incidental. It was her sense of childlike *play*, her joy in using this miracle of the telephone that most of us take for granted, that caused customers to seek her out.

"Many of these people who called us to place orders spent hours on the phone each day doing business. Probably, most of the voices they had to deal with over the phone were just that– impersonal, disembodied voices. What a pleasant relief it was for them to be able to do business with someone like Joan. It was like taking a break to chat with a friend– a real person at the other end, *and being able to take care of business at the same time.* "

* * *

It was so simple, I wondered why I had never thought of that. I was always so concerned with getting to the point, with taking care of business, it never even occurred to me to be chatty... interested in the life of the person on the other end of the line. I know I always enjoyed it when someone seemed to take a special interest in *me*, I thought.

"You know, JD, you just reminded me of my Uncle Dan. Because he lived in Florida, we only got to see him every five years or so, but he would call often, especially on birthdays and holidays. Other relatives called, but Uncle Dan's calls were always special. He made a point of remembering all our hobbies and favorite school subjects. Whenever he called, we would all bunch up around the phone waiting for our turn. Just hearing his voice felt like we were getting a big warm hug.

"Uncle Dan often described life in Florida over the phone. When he talked about taking a stroll at sunset on the boardwalk, we were able to smell the salt air in our New York apartment. Or when he told us of a fishing cruise he had taken we could *see* the blue of the sky and the ocean."

"Now you're cooking, Bob. Your Uncle Dan was a natural communicator who understood the telephone as a magical tool to cut through the illusion of distance."

"You see Bob, over the phone, **we can do things that would be impossible in person**. Illusions are created, images formed. For example, you can sound taller, thinner, or more successful than you really are. How many times have you been surprised by someone's appearance after first speaking with them on the phone?"

"Often."

"It's because you had formed an image based on what their words and voice tone were projecting over the phone. Your imagination is using someone else's words to paint a picture uniquely your own. In this *Let your fingers do the walking, Reach out and touch someone, Don't write, call* society of ours, learning to master this ultimate high-tech tool is essential to our success. Every part of our lives—business, personal and yes, even spiritual—depends on it."

"I think I'm starting to get the picture," I commented.

JD laughed. "Right now, with the right techniques and a little luck, you can reach ANYONE in the world. *The world is a push-button away.* Years ago, there was a story in the paper of a twelve year old who misdialed a number, got President John F. Kennedy on the phone and had a twenty minute conversation with him. JFK had great phone skills. And he very often answered the phone himself. That was a phone strategy that he found worked for *him.* And that is a conversation the young girl will remember for the rest of her life.

"Once you learn to master the telephone, it will transform your life, and give you a sense of power and artistry. You'll learn how to charm, enchant, humor, cajole, purr, flatter, mesmerize. You can use the phone for a last minute restaurant reservation, a hot seat at a Yankees game, money for an important project, to repair your daughter's broken heart, make a sale in New Zealand, make a date with someone special, heal a rift with a friend..."

JD was spellbinding. I was getting my own private seminar on *Re-Discovering the Magic of the Phone,* by a master communicator and teacher!

"When we stop to think about it, we are shocked how inextricably the phone has entwined itself into our lives, so subtle, so familiar that we take it for granted. We

"Each phone call can be viewed as an exciting adventure–a new story I've never heard before."

are no more amazed that Mom can call Dad to remind him to pick up a loaf of bread on his way home from work than we are that we can call our supplier in Hong Kong to ask why the latest shipment for our business has not arrived."

JD reached for his attache case, opened it and pulled out a newspaper clipping from *The New York Times*, "Phone Calls From the Fast Lane: Life Inside a Freeway Telephone Booth," and handed it to me. I began to read..."Robert Reinhold addresses the issue of the omnipresence of the telephone and how it is continuing to change our world.... many see a Copernican revolution in communication on the horizon... a second generation of light-weight portable and transportable phones is coming along... [introducing] a new age of 'personal communication'— a nightmare to some, perhaps— in which every person will have a 'universal' telephone number, reachable wherever he is, in the car, on the farm, on a boat, taking a walk."

"This sounds like my old phone nightmare."

"When you come over to pick up the other articles I mentioned earlier, you can get a copy of this one too, if you'd like. Why don't you give me your card in case you forget, and I can have my secretary send them to you.

"Remember, Bob, the phone was not always around. And because of that we had to accept the limitations of time and space. Now enhanced phone skills have given us the unlimited potential of a closer, more intimate world. We can 'reach out and touch someone' so they stay touched!"

"That's easy for you to say. You have that magic touch, that certain indescribable *knack.*"

"And," he said, as the captain requested that all passsengers buckle their belts for landing, "you can too, if you're willing to put in a little time studying my 'secrets.' I can give you a list of some very special people who might be able to help you fill in the missing pieces of your puzzle. Remind me to give you that list when you come by my office."

As JD began gathering his papers and putting them in his attache case, I quickly jotted down some notes to serve as a reminder of some of the points he had made during our conversation. I had no idea these first notes would be the beginning of this book about my strange telephone odyssey.

I had the oddest sensation when I finished my notes. It was as if I had been in some dark closet all my life and someone had just opened the door a crack. My eyes were still adjusting to the light. I could not have imagined then how I would be dazzled by the mysterious adventures that were to follow in the next months. And the funniest thing was that my old nemesis— the phone— was the key to it all.

* * *

O'RYAN'S PHONEMASTERY NOTES:

1) Restore *right attitude*— the feeling of *awe and wonder* of the phone. We've taken it for granted. Try to think of it as if you were seeing it for the first time, that it has just been invented.

2) *You can reach anyone in the world* quicker and have more intimate access than with any other means of communication available today.

3) The art of great phone skills can be learned, just like mastering a musical instrument.

4) Learn to make people feel you are interested in them, *who they are* and *how they feel,* not just the business you need to conduct over the phone.

5) Joan's secret: LISTEN well.

6) Each new phone call is a possible adventure. *Cultivate a sense of play and fun.* Business will happen naturally as an outcome of the call.

7) You can do things over the phone and create images that would be impossible in person.

* * *

CHAPTER TWO

IN WHICH I DISCOVER
THE THREE TYPES OF PHONERS

The Ear Phoner, The Eye Phoner
and the Feel Phoner

I don't know exactly why I did it, but after saying goodbye to JD, I headed straight to the nearest phone and called my wife. As my call was ringing through, I happened to notice JD in another phone booth and he gave me a 'thumbs up' sign. I smiled. Then my eight-year-old daughter, Lisa, answered the phone.

"Hello, this is Lisa."

"Hiya Mona Lisa," I said, using a favorite nickname. "It's Daddy."

"Oh, Daddy, where are you? We've been waiting for you."

"I'm at the airport, and I'll be home soon. I just wanted to hear my favorite girl's voice."

"We miss you!"

"I know, I've missed you too. Is mommy there?"

I heard Lisa holler through the house, "Mom, Dad's on the phone!"

"Bob?"

"Hi honey, I'm at the airport and I'll be home in

about an hour. But I also called just to let you know how much I love you and missed you."

"Bob, that's music to my ears. We missed you too. Especially Tommy, he's had a fever and been asking for you."

"Sounds serious."

"No, the doctor said it's just a flu. By the way, are you hungry? Should I have something ready for you?"

"No, honey, that's okay. I ate on the plane."

"You know I'm so glad you called. Is everything all right?"

"Yes, why do you ask?"

"Well, I know how much you hate telephone conversations and I can't remember when you called from the airport last."

"Everything is fine, really. I just felt like calling."

"Thanks, I really appreciate it. Can't wait to give you a big hug. You'd better go now or you'll miss the next bus."

"Okay, love ya. Be there soon."

I stood there for a moment amazed at my painless phone call. Sheryl was right. I rarely made this kind of a call. And that feeling I used to get in my stomach was gone. As a matter of fact I was beginning to feel excited about the possibilities. With so little effort— a couple of minutes on the telephone— I made my family happy and more secure. I felt better and it cost less than a dollar. I stared a few seconds at that black receiver in my hand and thought of what JD had said about having the whole world in your hands. I felt like I did for the first time in my life.

During the next week, I probably made more cold calls than I ever had in my life. I wasn't as afraid to pick up the phone and *use* it since my conversation on the airplane with JD. But, to my disappointment, I wasn't *that* much more successful in making appointments or selling new policies. I thought it might be time to take JD up on his offer to visit him at his office.

* * *

It wasn't as easy to get through to him as I assumed it would be. I called his office and got his secretary. And then I began to remember all the reasons I hated the telephone.

She had a nasal voice and in a business-like tone answered, "Mr. Deltone's office. May I help you?"

"Yes," I said, "I met JD on the plane back from the West Coast a week ago and I was wondering if I could talk to him to set up an appointment."

"Mr. Deltone is on a long distance call. Do you wish to hold?"

"No, that's okay," I said, and hung up. I hated being put on hold, especially if I had to listen to some kind of elevator music. I didn't know what to do with all that time.

I called several more times to speak with JD, and hung up quickly when I was told he was in a meeting or on another call. His secretary would always ask if I wanted to hold, but I always said no. I was upset because I realized my old phone phobias could still cause me to feel uncomfortable. Finally, I left my number and several hours later, JD returned my call.

"Hi Bob, how have you been? Sorry it took so long to get back to you."

"That's okay. I've been trying to get in touch with you for a week."

"Things have been really hopping around here. Why didn't you leave your name and number before?"

"I don't know."

"Sure you do, but we can go into that when we see each other."

"JD, I'd love to talk to you some more about the telephone. You mentioned coming by your office, but you seem busy. I..." I found myself trailing off lamely, not knowing how to finish the thought I had begun, and feeling apologetic.

"I am busy but one of the calls I returned before I called you back was a cancellation of my 3 o'clock appointment. How's that for you?" I looked down at my appointment book. There were two meetings scheduled.

"Listen, JD I have two appointments at that time. Let me call them and try to loosen up my schedule. I'll ring you right back."

"Okay. I'll tell Martha to put you through."

"Martha?"

"Yes, my secretary. Didn't you ask her name when you called all those times?"

"No, I guess I didn't."

"What a phonesnob you are," he said, chuckling.

"Guess so. But I'm sure by the time you're done with me I'll be a phonemaster."

"You bet!" he said in an enthusiastic voice. "Now you've got the attitude."

"Call you right back." I looked at my appointment book and figured out the calls I'd have to make to pry myself loose. I began to dread making the calls. Then something started to happen deep inside me. My anxiety turned to determination. I stared at the phone and began to talk to it. I hoped no one would walk into my office. They'd think I'd lost my marbles for sure. "I'm going to master you if it's the last thing I do, you &^%$*#."

At the time it seemed like luck that I was able to get through to everyone and reschedule our meetings. I also made it a point to ask the secretary his or her name and jotted them down in my personal phone book. I also took out my phone notes from the airplane, and added: "Always ask the name of the person you are talking to on the phone, even if it is not the person you are trying to reach. It's more personal." Then I thought a moment, and added, "In fact, it's just plain courteous. People are not machines."

* * *

I walked into the small reception area of JD's office at Transcom Satellites Inc. Martha looked up from her almost perfectly organized desk, took a tissue from one of several tissue boxes and blew her red, swollen nose. "How may I help you?"

"Hi, Martha, I'm Bob O'Ryan. JD is expecting me."

Nodding her head, she said, "He's on the phone and will be with you shortly," and motioned for me to take a seat. I could hear JD's deep laugh even through the office doors. He sure has fun on the phone, I thought. A photograph on the wall of a TransCom communication satellite circling the earth caught my eye. When Martha's buzzer sounded, she said, "You can go in now."

As I opened the door I gave Martha a smile and said, "Hope your cold gets better soon."

She sniffed and, for the first time smiled, "Thanks. I hope so too."

JD's office was a clutter of piles of papers, books, magazines, and bound reports. Photos, clippings, and notes covered several walls. There were archery trophies, pictures of his family, award plaques, etc. He walked from behind his desk with a warm smile and clasped my outstretched hand with both of his hands. "Good to see you, Bob. Have a seat."

His phone rang. "Excuse me please, I've been waiting for this important call. I'll just be a few minutes."

I started to wander around the room. His wall clutter was fascinating. One of the first things I noticed was a large index card with a hand-printed quote from Carl Rogers:

> *If I can <u>listen</u> to what he tells me,*
> *if I can <u>understand</u> how it seems to him,*
> *if I can <u>sense</u> the <u>emotional</u> flavor*
> *which it has for him,*
> *then I will be releasing potent forces*
> *of change within him.*

JD had underscored certain words on the frayed and yellow card; he must have had it for a long time. Next to this was another small, framed quote by Arnold Toynbee. It said:

> *To get to know each other on a world-wide scale is the human race's most urgent need today.*

As I was scanning his wall, I could hear him on the phone. God, was he smooth. Smooth is the wrong word, actually, because that has a kind of slick or manipulative tone to it. He was caring, *genuinely* caring. And he listened a lot. He knew the names of the wife and children, and the concerns of whomever was on the other end of the line. It sounded like a social call, until close to the end, when I overheard him repeating a product order back to the caller. The business deal didn't seem to be the thing he was concentrating on, it seemed more like an after-thought.

After hanging up, he buzzed Martha and asked her to hold all calls. I noticed three small cartoons next to his telephone. He must have noticed me staring at them, because as I sat down, he picked up the frame and handed it to me. "An artist friend of mine drew these for me. Aren't they great?"

There were three people in the cartoons. One of the characters had exaggerated eyes, five times larger than normal. The next had huge ears, twice as big as his feet. The third had enormous hands, each the size of his head. Underneath each it said respectively, **Eye Phoner, Ear Phoner, Feel Phoner**.

"What are these?"

"They are reminders to me to listen well. No, that's not right, they are reminders to me on *how* to listen well."

"You mentioned the same thing on the plane. You said that one of the secrets of good phone skills was listening."

"That's right. As matter of fact, I ran across a great quote the other day as I was reading *In Search of Excellence: Lessons From America's Best-Run Companies*." He reached for the pile of books on his desk and pulled one out. There were little pieces of paper sticking out of the top. He turned to one, and with the excitement of a miner finding gold, read aloud:

"...the excellent companies are not only better on service, quality, reliability and finding a niche. *They are also better listeners....* The fact that these companies are so strong on quality, service, and the rest comes in large measure from *paying attention* to what customers want. *From listening."* (italics are JD's emphasis)

"Yup," he said closing the book. "Listening well is what it's all about. And remember, we are not just talking about business communication here. We're talking about all communication— housewives, C.E.O.'s, adolescents, relatives, salespeople, telephone operators, telemarketing experts, volunteers on crisis 'hotlines', social workers, dentists, editors, receptionists, elevator operators, busdrivers, conductors... the list is endless. The common thread is they all need to communicate. How we reach out is largely responsible for what comes in, whether we are talking about love, respect, orders, profits, fun or understanding.... even spiritual enlightenment."

"Ever since our conversation on the airplane, I've noticed I have a new respect for the phone and the power of communication. But I realize I need a lot more, so I thought I would take you up on your offer. I've made you my offical *Phoneguru."*

"I'm honored. I've been called a lot of things in my life, but never that."

We both laughed.

"So," I reminded him, "what do these cartoons mean?"

"Oh, yes. I do tend to wander. These are the three types of phoners you might encounter— **The Eye Phoner, The Ear Phoner,** and **the Feel Phoner.**"

"It's possible for me to take care of business over the phone and at the same time be having fun. In fact, my business will run more smoothly."

"Aren't people more complex than that?"

"Of course, but these are **useful generalities**. Once you understand them, you can play more complicated *tunes* with your phoneskills. You see, when two people are in rapport, as we are now, listening becomes effortless. I know you're interested in me, and don't mind me running-at-the-mouth or making my silly puns. So I feel *relaxed* with you. When I speak to you, I try to do it in such a way as to make you want to listen. And vice-versa. In good communication both people get the feeling they are **speaking the same language**. Getting that feeling is the very foundation of communication and phone excellence."

"JD," I said, "I haven't the faintest idea how this relates to those cartoons."

"Just relax, you'll get it. Most rapport is built on the recognition of 'sameness.' People feel closest to other people like themselves. You can hear it in the way they describe people they become friendly with:*We see eye-to-eye, We just speak the same language, I just feel comfortable around them because they are so easy to be with*, are common phrases. We, consciously or unconsciously, **mirror** back to another that we are enough like them to understand what they are saying.

"For instance, I might be talking about my children, and you, also being a parent, might validate my experience by saying something like *I have two kids, too, and I know exactly what you mean!*

"There are several ways to mirror," he said, rapidly spilling out information with the enthusiasm of a little boy, "the way you dress, your hobby or sport, beliefs (religious, political or philosophical), common experiences (the army, college fraternity) etc. These are the building blocks, the foundation, upon which good friend-

ships, rapport, phone and communication excellence are built. Some of the actual construction is done with words. But the information about our *sameness* is communicated not only by what we say but **how we say them.** Understand?"

"Sort of," I answered.

"If I were to look at you with an angry expression on my face and yelled that I loved you, how would you feel?"

"That you were angry at me."

"Even if the words were 'I love you?'"

"Yes."

"Right! Some researchers estimate that only **7 percent** of the information is conveyed through words, **38 percent** through tone of voice. The remaining **55 percent** is transmitted through our body language. Since telephone conversations are devoid of the last **55 percent** of this information, it becomes even more important to make the most of the *tone, volume, tempo, and timbre* used while speaking."

JD reached into his pile of books and handed me another one, this one was called *Sound Medicine*, by Laeh Maggie Garfield. "Take a look at that," JD suggested. It fell open to where a bookmark was inserted. Heavily underlined passages jumped out at me:

> *The tonal quality of our speech tells more about us, on a subtle level, than the words we say. A great part of our personality comes through the voice... The healthy person has a well-modulated, clear, rich voice that is kind in tone and word. The wispy voice of a shy person, the cracking voice of someone in fear or under tremendous stress, and the booming tones of someone who is trying to put one over*

on you are all dead giveaways. The rounded, sonorous sounds of a person who believes sincerely in their projects and follows their inner light is quite different from the indwelling abrasiveness of the super salesman who only wants you in their grasp 'til the money is delivered.

I had never heard it put just that way! The last part described just what I was thinking earlier, about what set JD's conversation apart from the usual sales pitch. I had always considered myself a pretty practical guy; this felt a little bit like mystical mumbo jumbo, but maybe JD *was* following an "inner light."

While I reviewed this new information and the chain of thoughts it set off, JD continued speaking with no dimming of enthusiasm. The man's energy was contagious. He was so passionately involved in what he was saying!

"If what the researchers and pioneers in this dynamic new field say is true, that people *do* speak in different languages, what should we be *listening for* so we can reply in their own personal and favorite mode of communication and *capture their ear?* How can we establish instantaneous rapport and dramatically increase our communication effectiveness so when the time comes *they want to listen to us* ?"

I shrugged theatrically and said "I give up." JD didn't miss a beat.

"If you begin to listen closely to people you will easily start noticing everyday figures of speech that are clear indicators of their preferred and most-used 'language': 'Yes, I *see* what you mean.' 'Now I get the *picture.*' 'You know, that name *rings a bell* with me.' 'Sure, dinner *sounds* good to me.' 'I really don't *feel comfortable* about that.' 'Good idea. Let's stay *in touch* about it.'

"Go on. This is fascinating!"

"And there's more," he said proudly. "We navigate through life using our senses, taking in information about the world around us by what we *see* (VISUAL), what we *hear* (AUDITORY) and what we *feel* (KINES-THETIC). Though we use all three of these neurological systems, research indicates we each have our favorite: the one we like to depend on or use the most. It's like our preference for using our right or left hand for doing tasks."

I interrupted him at that point. "What do you think I am, JD, auditory, visual or kinesthetic?"

"Bob, pay attention to what you say. Listen to which phrases you often use in conversation. It will be far more rewarding for you to discover what type you are, than for me to tell you. Discovery is the spark of learning. Anyway, let me continue, and it will become clearer. If a person can speak Italian, Greek, or French, and you can speak all three languages, wouldn't it make sense to talk to them in *their* preferred language?"

"Of course."

"Wouldn't it make them feel more at home and give them the feeling that you're *just like them*?"

"Yes."

"Presto, you've established rapport." JD handed me a few sheets of typed pages from his desk, saying, "Here are some notes I've had xeroxed on the three types of phoners. You can take them with you to study later. They may help you figure out your type."

Then he pulled a folded sheet of stationery out of his jacket pocket and put it on top of the notes in my hand. "Here is a list of people who I have worked with or consider to be phonegurus— if that's what you'd like to call them. You'll find that when you speak to these people, each will give you a piece of the puzzle. If you have any questions on this material, just give me a call."

"JD, this might be a stupid question. But why are you doing all this for me? I mean, this is a lot of time and material you are sharing. What do you get out of all this?"

He stopped and thought for a moment, drifting off into private memories, and then said "Bob, you remind me of how I used to be. Of how I was before I learned that by helping one person, I help the world." And as an afterthought he added, "And I also owe something. This is my way of repaying someone who changed my life. That person, by the way, is not on the list I just gave you. You can't find him. He's very private. But maybe, just maybe, you'll bump into him."

"Sounds mysterious to me!"

"More than you'll ever know, Bob. More than you'll ever know."

* * *

JD'S PHONE NOTES:

The Eye Phoner (Visual Person)

Let's *face it,* the Eye Phoner or Visually oriented person would prefer a face-to-face conversation to talking over the phone. Phone conversations make them a bit uneasy since they can't use their favorite method of getting information, like checking out facial expressions and posture.

In matters of love, for example, a visual person needs to be *shown* how much they mean to you. You could *tell* them until you're blue in the face, it just won't register. You're not on their "wavelength."

If you have someone on the other end of the phone who speaks rapidly (they are trying to keep pace with the pictures in their head), most likely they are an Eye Phoner. It's not only *what* a person says, it's *how* they say it. The tone they use will be high pitched and have a nasal or somewhat strained quality to it. The tempo will be in quick bursts of words, sometimes continuing until they come up for air. They are the fast talkers.

There are other clues in addition to what and how they say things. If their profession is that of a painter, photographer, interior designer, hair dresser, publisher, editor, manuscript reader, makeup artist, etc.— predominately *visual* activities—you may have an Eye Phoner on the other end of the line. For example, if you are trying to sell them a car, you'll know that the most important thing to them is how it *looks*— not how it sounds, how plush the interior feels, or how it handles on the road.

Additional clues can be picked up by finding out what their hobbies are, how they spend their free time. They love reading, watching television, going to the movies, shopping, decorating, collecting things like stamps, antique cars, painted eggs, etc. Are you starting to get the picture?

The following is a partial list of phrases and words your Eye Phoner will tend to use:

Analyze	An eyeful	Angle
Appears to me	Appear	Aspect
Beyond a shadow of a doubt	Bird's eye view	Blackness
Bright	Catch a glimpse of	Clarity
Clear	Clear as day	Clear-cut
Cognizant	Colorful	Conspicuous
Demonstrate	Dim view	Dream
Enlighten	Examine	Eyeful
Flashed on	Focus	Foresee
Fuzzy	Get a perspective on	Get a scope on
Glance	Glimpse	Gray
Hazy	Hazy idea	Hindsight
Horse of a different color	Horizon	Idea
Illusion	Image	Imagine
In light of	In person	Inspect
In view of	Look	Looks like
Make a scene	Mental image	Mental picture
Mind's Eye	Naked eye	Notice
Obscure	Observe	Ogle
Outlook	Paint a picture	Peek
Perception	Perspective	Picture
Photographic memory	Pinpoint	Plainly see
Pretty	Pretty as a picture	Preview
Scene	Scope	Scrutinize
See	See to it	Seem
Short-sighted	Show	Showing off
Sight	Sight for sore eyes	Sketch
Sketchy	Staring off into space	Survey
Take a peek	Tunnel vision	Under your nose
Up front	Vague	View
Vision	Vivid	Watch
Well defined	Witness	

Now things are probably clearer than ever, and you can start to respond to your Eye Phoner in their preferred mode or "language" in order to establish rapport and let them know they are really being listened to and understood. These are just a few samples:

SPOKEN	A RAPPORT REPLY
That proposal seems *vague* to me.	Perhaps I can *shed some more light* on it.
Do you get the *picture?*	Yes, I *see* just what you mean.
The longer I *look at* this, the more puzzled I get.	We need to put the problem *in better focus.*
It *appears* that we are headed for a *bright* future.	That's my *perception* exactly.
She was such a *colorful* character.	Hearing you describe her, I can get a *clear mental picture.*
I *foresee* a good future with our new partner.	It certainly *seems* like we *see eye-to-eye* on that subject.

* * *

The Ear Phoner (Auditory Person)

The Ear Phoners like to hear themselves talk. They love talking on the telephone and can do so for long periods of time. If you have the occasion to *explain* to an auditory person how to do something, better not try to show them how, they'll want you to *tell them* how.

Ear Phoners are very easy to recognize. They have rhythmic, resonant voices, which seem to emanate from deeper in their chest, as opposed to Eye Phoners, who

mostly speak from their throat. They speak slower than Eye Phoners (who rush along like there is no tomorow), and have a "melodious" distinctive tone of voice. Ear Phoners become irritated quickly by loud, unharmonious sounds. Don't shout at them or use a shrill tone if you want them to listen. They are generally articulate, taking great pains to express themselves well. Richard Burton, Eleanor Roosevelt, Barbara Walters, Orson Welles, John Kennedy, William F. Buckley, and Jerry Brown are a few examples.

Ear Phoners understand the world around them by how things *sound,* so of course they will use words in their communication which reflect that mode of perception. They'll use phrases like "I *hear* what you're *saying,*" or "That *sounds* good to me," In a phone conversation with an Ear Phoner about their summer vacation at the beach most of their comments and descriptions will center around the *sounds.*

"Oh, what a *harmonious* time we had at the seashore. The *sound* of the surf and the *calls* of the seagulls were so relaxing I wished we could have stayed another week instead of returning to this *noisy* city." As the auditory person was raving about the sounds of the beach, their visually oriented partner might have been exclaiming about how the beach *looked,* "Oh, those *colors* in the clouds. *See* them! The reds and pinks and lavender. Oh God, what a *sight!* "

Ear Phoners pay attention to diction and take their time pronouncing each word. There is an unmistakable resonance, a distinctive voice, greater spacing between the words and calculated pauses that let their words seem to hang in the air. They are our great public speakers, radio announcers, singers, musicians, lawyers, debators, teachers, sound engineers, as well as possibly stereo sales or repair people.

They love to fill their free time with sound: going to concerts, talking on the telephone or C.B. radios, playing musical instruments, listening to lectures, talking to themselves, eavesdropping on other poeple's conversations or gossiping.

The following is a partial list of phrases and words Ear Phoners are fond of using and with which their sentences will be peppered. Notice they all, in one way or another, have to do with sound:

After-thought	Announce	Articulate
Audible	Blabber-mouth	Boisterous
Call	Call on	Clash
Clear as a bell	Clearly expressed	Click
Communicate	Converse	Crashing
Describe in detail	Discuss	Dissonant
Divulge	Earful	Earshot
Enunciate	Express yourself	Give an account of
Give me your ear	Gossip	Grant an audience
Harmony	Hear	Heard voices
Hidden message	Hold your tongue	Hum
Hush	Idle talk	Inquire
Inquire into	Interview	Keynote speaker
Listen	Loud	Loud and clear
Manner of speaking	Mellifluous	Mention
Noise	Noisy	Oral
Outspoken	Pay attention to	Power of speech
Proclaim	Pronounce	Purrs like a kitten
Quiet	Rap session	Remark
Report	Ring	Rings a bell
Roar	Rumor	Say
Scream	Screech	Shout
Shrill	Silence	Sing
Sound	Speak	Speechless
Squeal	State	State your purpose
Talk	Tattle-tale	Tell
Tinkling	Thunderous	Told

Tone	Tongue-tied	To tell the truth
Tune, tune up	Unheard of	Utter
Vocal	Voice	Voiced an opinion
Well-informed	Within hearing range	Word for word
Yell		

Now that you can recognize an Ear Phoner when you hear one, look over the following samples of what they might say and how to reply to them to achieve maximum effectiveness in your communication and listening skills:

SPOKEN	A RAPPORT REPLY
It doesn't *sound* like such a reasonable request to me.	In a *manner of speaking* you're correct.
There was such *harmony* at the office.	I'll *say!*
As soon as she walked into the room I was *tongue-tied*.	I *hear* you.
Did you detect a *hidden message?*	I did hear something in the *tone of his voice.*
The *noise* level in that class-room makes it difficult to *pay attention to* the teacher.	I'll *tell* you! It's enough to make you *scream!*

*　*　*

The Feel Phoner (Kinesthetic Person)

I'd like to give you a real *feel* for how the Feel Phoner gets a *grip* on reality, how they make sense of the world around them on the basis of their feelings. They

"How I say something over the phone is far more important than what I am saying. Communication is 7 percent words, 38 percent tone of voice, and 55 percent non-verbal."

understand what you say by what they feel when you say it. To that kind of phone caller the maxim, "It's not *what* you say, but *how* you say it," is especially applicable.

Decisions are therefore based on whether they feel good. They depend on *gut* intuition.

Don't expect any long, verbal explanations because the Feel Phoner finds it hard to put his or her feelings into words, and as they struggle, there will be lots of deep sighs. They expect you to get a ten thousand word message of comfort in a gentle pat on the hand. Sometimes it works, particularly if the other person is Kinesthetically oriented. Otherwise it is an empty gesture to a visual or auditory person.

There are very long pauses when you ask them whether or not they want to go to the movies. They hem and haw as they try to transpose their feeling into words that auditory or visual people might understand. They rely primarily on metaphors that are physically anchored in the real world: body-based sensations of feelings, emotions, smell and taste.

A walk on the beach with a kinesthetic would center around how the sand *feels* between their toes, how the salt water spray *smells*, how the breeze on their face and the warmth of your arm makes their stomach *feel* as if it were full of butterflies, their head dizzy with joy. Do you have a good *hold* on this concept? The most significant thing you can say to a Feel Phoner is "I understand how you feel." The words alone aren't enough; without feeling behind them they will seem empty.

Generally they have occupations like carpenter, sculptor, hairdresser, physical therapist, dentist, surgeon, psychologist, cook, aerobics instructor, dance teacher, masseur, or athletic coach. In their spare time they might like to smoke, dance, drink, eat, sail, scuba

dive, run, weight lift, swim, walk, make love a lot, lie in the sun, take long hot baths, etc.

Their speech patterns exhibit a very slow tempo with very long pauses. The words often seem to be bubbling up slowly from the region of their abdomen. The kind of phrase and words they use are unmistakable. Here is a sample list:

Active	Affected	All washed up
Bearable	Bind	Boils down to
Break	Callous	Charge
Cold	Come to grips with	Concrete
Control yourself	Cool	Cool/calm/collected
Dig	Emotional	Feel
Firm	Firm foundation	Float
Floating on thin air	Flow	Foundation
Freeze	Get a handle on	Get a load of this
Get in touch with	Get the drift of	Get your goat
Grasp	Grip	Hand-in-hand
Handle	Hang in there!	Hanging
Hassle	Heated	Heated arguments
Hold	Hold it!	Hold on!
Hot-head	Hunch	Hurt
Hustle	Intuition	Know-how
Lay cards on table	Light-headed	Lukewarm
Moment of panic	Motion	Muddled
Nail	Not following you	Painful
Pain-in-the-neck	Panicky	Pounding
Pressure	Pull some strings	Push
Rough	Rush	Scratch
Sensitive	Set	Shallow
Sharp as a tack	Shift	Slipped my mind
Smooth operator	Softy	Solid
So-so	Sore	Squeeze
Stiff upper lip	Stir	Stress
Stretch	Structured	Stuffed shirt
Support	Tension	Tied up
Too much a hassle	Touch	Topsy-turvy
Unbearable	Underhanded	Unravel
Unsettled	Warm	Wring

How would you respond to a Feel Phoner for maximum results? Get in touch with these sample dialogues:

SPOKEN	A RAPPORT REPLY
I *feel* comfortable around my new boss.	I had a *hunch* that you felt that way.
She just wasn't able to *get a grip* on herself.	Sometimes it can be very difficult for a *sensitive* person under that kind of *pressure.*
Being caught in traffic really *shook me up.*	It's important to *keep your shirt on* in those situations.
I envy her. She's always so *cool, calm, and collected.*	Yes, but maybe she's not *in touch* with her *feelings.*
It's just too *heavy* for me to deal with.	Perhaps we can *walk through* the problem over the phone.

* * *

It is important to remember that **people do use all three systems.** When in doubt, use the "shotgun" method—use all three. For example, for a real estate sale: "The house, Mr. Jones, is just what you are looking for. It has elegant woodwork, a white picket fence, and it's located in a picturesque neighborhood, on a quiet street far from any noise of traffic. You'll be so comfortable there. You'll just have to feel it to believe it. Are you free this afternoon?"

Now how can you miss?

The amazing thing is, after familiarizing yourself with these new concepts, you'll find that you are comfortable with any of the three general types of phoners and can move in and out of their preferred mode of communication easily, elegantly, naturally, and with grace.

It becomes second nature, which is the goal. You certainly don't want to be trying to listen and at the same time worrying, "Oh, dear. Is he an Eye Phoner. No. Sounds like an Ear phoner. Maybe not. I'm just not good at this, it makes me confused." **Trust yourself.** Trust that after reading this and a little practice, the information will have changed you into a more effective and powerful communicator, mastering the Art of the Telephone.

* * *

O'RYAN'S PHONEMASTERY NOTES:

1) When you pick up the phone, remember you have the whole world in your hands. Even putting a sticker of Earth on it will help remind you. They are now sold in most novelty/gift stores.

2) Avoid being a *phonesnob.* Always get the name of the person with whom you are speaking, even if you called for someone else. It's more personal and courteous. People are not machines.

3) Potent forces of change are released in other people by you *listening well.* Be genuinely caring about the person on the other end of the line. Be interested in other people. Everyone has their story. Even if you think they are just average and possibly could not have any-

thing interesting to say, a majority of the time you'll be wrong and have missed out on a potentially delightful experience.

4) There are three types of telephoners: **Eye Phoner** (visual), **Ear Phoner** (auditory), **Feel Phoner** (kinesthetic). You can learn to "speak the same language" when communicating with someone and have profound results.

5) Researchers in communication have revealed that it is *not what we say* as much as it is *how we say it*. 7 percent of information is conveyed through words, 38 percent through tone of voice, 55 percent through body language. Since phone communication is not face-to-face, the first two are the most important. Voice tone and inflection can reveal far more than words.

6) No matter how pressured you are, act as if you have *all the time in the world* when you are on the phone. If it is an emergency, say so.

7) If you are in doubt about what kind of phoner you are speaking with, just trust yourself. You'll be surprised.

8) Remember, **the three classifications of phoners are only useful generalities. Everyone uses all three systems** but does have a preferred mode just like you have two hands but favor one. The right or left hand dominates.

CHAPTER THREE

PRETENDING TO BE NATURAL

Or, How I Learned To Be A Good Phoney

With the new information I had gotten from JD, I felt sure I had found *the* secret to phonemastery. So, people spoke in different languages! As the train pulled out of the station I headed home filled with enthusiasm and new tools. God, it made so much sense! If you wanted to establish rapport with someone, of course you'd speak to them in French if they spoke French and you could too. It was just as JD pointed out, common courtesy!

I couldn't wait to tell Sheryl. I was so sure she'd be excited about it too. She loves to learn new things. She is forever going to seminars of all kinds and is convinced it is what keeps her so young looking and alive. Her enthusiasm is one of the many reasons I married her. Everyone seems to like her, they say she is such a good listener. I can vouch for that because there was many a time I took her up on that "it's-ok-to-lean-on-me" look of hers. I just couldn't wait to talk to her and share my excitement about the new information and tools.

I couldn't have been more disappointed.

* * *

It was Friday night, and as usual, the kids were over at Grandma's getting their weekly dose of being spoiled. During the train ride I thought over what JD had suggested. I was trying to figure out whether Sheryl was a **Eye, Ear,** or **Feel Phoner.** It might be easier to start with figuring out what someone else close to me was, before I decided on my own classification!

It wasn't long before I realized my wife is forever talking about feelings. She always tells me I don't talk about my feelings very much. So I was ready when I walked through the door to talk to her in kinesthetic terms.

"Hi honey," I said in a deeper voice than normal, and then as I was hugging her, I said, "Oh, sweetie, it's so good to *feel* you in my arms!"

She pushed me away and with a quizzical look on her face, replied, "What have you been up to, mister?"

I laughed nervously. "What do you mean?"

"What's wrong, don't you understand the English language? What have you been up to?" Then pointing to her mouth she said, "Read my lips!"

"Nothing, I've been at JD's all afternoon."

"I know that, you told me over the phone. You sound different. Like you're hiding something. I can feel it."

"There it is," I thought to myself. "She is kinesthetic!" So I remembered one of the **Feel Phoner** phrases and answered. "Well, let me take my coat off and try and get in touch with what you are feeling."

"What *is* going on? Now, I'm sure of it! You never talk like this. Are you trying to be Phil Donohue?"

Well, I just had to laugh. I plopped down on the couch and told her all about my conversation with JD, and explained as best I could the different languages people spoke. I pulled the pages JD had given me out of my briefcase and showed her. She looked down at them, pushing her long brown hair out of her face.

"This is interesting," she said, "but I don't think it's going to make you a better communicator, especially over the phone."

Boy, did she take the wind out of my sails!

Feeling defensive, I said, "Well, you're good on the phone. What do you think the secret is?"

Sheryl must have noticed the wounded look on my face (sometimes I can bruise easily). She got up from her favorite lounging chair in the living room, and came over and sat down close to me on the couch. She patted my knee and kissed me on the cheek. "I'm sorry, you've had a long day— let's have something to eat," she said, starting to get up.

"Just a minute," I said, "Please answer my question. What do you think the most important thing is in good communication? And I don't care whether it's on the phone or face-to-face!"

Sheryl got a pensive look on her face and then, a few moments later, replied, "Well, I'm not really sure, but whatever it is, it's got to be natural."

"Natural?"

"Natural," she repeated with a gentle smile. She kissed me again and said, "Read my lips, n-a-t-u-r-a-l."

"I don't understand," I conceded.

"I think the last thing you want to do is to come off as if you are using a technique. People will get turned off faster than a neon sign in a thunderstorm!"

"But JD said it works for lots of people!"

"Yes, but what is a blessing for one person can be a curse for another. Not everything works for everybody all the time under all conditions."

"That's brilliant," I said and immediately took my notebook out from my attache case and wrote it down in my phone notes.

"See, there you go, trying to memorize a technique. It's like trying to wear someone else's clothes. You can model your style of dressing after someone else's, but their clothes will never be a perfect fit for you. Put away your notebook, just relax, and be yourself. People can feel it if you're pretending. They'll pick up on it immediately."

"Yes," I chimed in, "JD said sort of the same thing. That human communication is ten percent verbal and ninety percent non-verbal; that it's more important *how* you say something, not necessarily *what* you say."

"You can't pretend sincerity. That's what I'm saying! I'm not sure what JD means. But I can tell you something about yourself."

"What's that?" I asked.

"Remember I love you and I'm just trying to help. Darling, you're trying too hard. You are great just the way you are. Stop trying so hard and you'll do fine. You'll even be able to use JD's phone techniques and not sound like you are copying someone else. You'll just be you. Trust me! Or else you are telling me I have poor judgement. After all, I chose to marry you! Now you wouldn't want to insult me would you?"

I smiled back at her, "No, I wouldn't!"

"Good, now let me go warm up dinner, we'll both feel better after we've had something to eat."

We decided to watch an old 1940's movie starring Cary Grant while we ate. It was one of our favorite things to do. Now, there is a smooth talker. So natural. So effortless. He makes it look so easy!

During the movie, Sheryl feel asleep with her head on my shoulder. So much for Cary Grant's ability to keep

"Learning telephone skills is a process, not an event. There will never be a time when I have finished perfecting them."

a person awake! I gently moved her head, got up, and covered her with Gran's afghan blanket. I needed to talk to JD. I was confused. As I dialed, I wondered if it was okay to call him at home at nine o'clock on a Friday night. I should have trusted my instincts.

He picked up the phone and there was that now familiar, warm "Hello?"

"Bob O'Ryan here, JD. I need to talk to you. Is this a convenient time?"

JD sounded preoccupied. "Well, it really isn't. I have to leave shortly." There was a short silence and just as I was going to apologize for calling him at home at that hour, he said, in a slightly friendlier tone of voice, "but we can talk until then."

I explained what had happened since I came home and told Sheryl about the three types of phoners.

JD listened attentively as I spoke and when I was done replied, "Son, I've got good news and bad news for you. Which do you want first?"

"I'll take the bad first."

"Spoken like a true pessimist," he said laughing. "I'll give you the worst first. Sheryl's right."

"Okay, what's the good news?"

"She's wrong!" he said with exactly the same emphasis.

Now I was totally confused! "Come on, JD, I've had a hard night. What are you talking about?"

"Now, now, my boy, you haven't had a hard night. What is happening in the Sudan or Bangladesh is a hard night. You're a little confused, that's all."

"Well, I'm trying real hard to put into practice what you've taught me."

"That's admirable, but you're trying too hard."

"That's what Sheryl said."

"And that's why I said she was right."

"Oh?"

"Listen. You're doing great. Don't worry so much. Relax."

"Easy for you to say."

"Yup."

There was a moment of silence on the phone.

"JD?"

"Yes, I'm here."

"Help," I yelled in a mock scream.

"Sheryl has hit upon one of the most important aspects of good phone skills. You have to sound natural, *congruent* is the word we use. Otherwise you'll sound false; what you are saying won't 'ring true.' Though what she doesn't realize is that 'pretending' can be one of the most powerful tools available to anyone integrating new behaviors."

"I didn't quite follow that, come again?"

"Just hold on a minute," he said. There was silence on the phone. It irked me— I still hated being put on hold.

It was several minutes before he returned to the phone and said, "This is from an article that appeared in the January 1987 issue of *Psychology Today.* It's about an experiment conducted in Britain in which a group of learning-disabled children aged 6 to 10 worked on problems from the Matching Familiar Figures (MFF) test. According to the article, a British psychologist, Robert Hartley, asked the students, while they were working on the test, to pretend that they were very intelligent and clever. The results were amazing.

"In summary, the learning-disabled children did as well as the previously better scorers on the test. When told of their superior performance, one of the children said, 'That wasn't me. I was only pretending to be smart.

I'm really stupid.' Isn't that amazing?

"One can pretend their way to the top! In other words, be, do, think, act, feel, dress, move, talk, and walk *as if* you already have the thing you want and the resources within you will be tapped that will actually make it come true. This works because the body/mind doesn't know the difference between what is real or imagined. You'll see it when you believe it."

"I don't understand."

"Well, unless you *stretch* beyond what has become habitual for you, the rut you run, you'll never grow. Throw yourself into a new situation and you'll discover things about yourself, strengths and talents, you never even dreamed of before. As matter of fact, I have a great idea. Do you have the list of names of the phone masters I gave you?"

"Yes, it's right here."

"Good. Go see the first person on the list. Her name is Milly, and she works at the Hotline. She also happens to be my eldest daughter."

* * *

O'RYAN'S PHONEMASTERY NOTES:

1) Above all phone techniques you may acquire in your life, be natural.

2) Be patient with yourself when learning anything new. New information takes some time to integrate. Don't try too hard. Learning is a process, not an event.

3) Because the body/mind doesn't know the difference between what is real or imagined, you can be anything you want. **You'll see it when you believe it.**

4) Being, doing, thinking, acting, dressing, walking, talking, and feeling **AS IF** you already have the thing you want fires off the necessary neurology necessary to elicit the new behavioral pattern.

5) Modelling other people's behavior is what we do from the time we are infants. It is a very powerful tool when used consciously. There isn't anything you can't do that another human being has done.

6) If you say one thing and do another, you're not congruent.

7) Remember, **not everything works for everybody in every situation.** If you are not getting the response you want, use any other tool, technique, or strategy than the one you've been using. It's just common sense.

CHAPTER FOUR

HOW TO BE COOL
WITH A HOT PHONE

As I walked up the porch steps to the small two-story gray frame building, I noticed a bulletin board covered with numerous hand-written notices announcing rides going west, help wanted, services offered, apartments for rent, animals for free, roommates wanted, and various items for sale or free. In the fading light of early evening, I could see that all of them ended with phone numbers. "Ah, the ubiquitous phone, in every walk of life," I thought to myself.

Inside the brightly lit room, a long table stretched from wall to wall, blocking off one section of the room from the rest. Behind it sat three people, all with telephones to their ears.

This was definitely the Hotline, where JD's daughter, Milly, worked as a volunteer twice a week. It was the first stop on the list JD had given me. A large sign above the long table said **"Technique is what you fall back on when you run out of inspiration."** Underneath the quote was the name R. Nureyev. Was he a Fortune 500 exec? As I was trying to place the name, I looked at the woman closest to me.

She had a round face and salt and pepper hair pulled back in a bun. There were deep smile lines at the

corners of her eyes. She was talking on the phone, "Okay,
Jason, now that we've had a chance to look at some of
those areas that were bothering you, perhaps you can
think about some of the different ways that you might be
able to share what you've discovered with your parents.
Yes, of course they can call me."

As she listened attentively for a minute she glanced
up and grinned at me, then spoke again into the phone.
"You did the right thing by calling the Hotline. If you need
to talk to someone again, please call us. That's what we're
here for. And it doesn't matter if it's the middle of the
night... Whenever you need someone to talk to, or just to
listen to you, give us a call. Okay?"

She listened to the phone for a few more seconds.
"Oh, you want to talk about *that* now? Okay. Just hold
on while I move to a more comfortable chair. This sounds
like we might need to take some extra time with it. So I'm
going to put you on hold, but stay right there, I'll pick up
again in one minute."

Pushing down the hold button and brushing a few
strands of hair that had gotten loose back from her
forehead, the woman looked up and grinned at me again.
It was infectious. I found myself grinning back.

"Hi, can I help you?"

"Yes, I hope so. I'm looking for Milly Deltone."

"Milly's in the middle of a call. I'm not sure how long
she'll be busy. Is it urgent? Perhaps someone else can
help you."

"No, it's not an emergency or anything like that...
I could just sit here and wait for a few minutes and see if
she gets free. If that's all right."

"Of course it is. My name's Paula Zbnewski... yes,
I know, what's a nice Japanese woman like me doing with
a handle like that? Well, it's a long story, but you can call

me Paula or PZ, everybody else does–'Easy PZ!' Now, I'll just write a short note to Milly— that's her, in the corner, on the green phone— and slip it to her so she knows you're waiting for her. What's your name?"

All of this was said so rapid-fire that it took me a moment to realize that there was a question I had to answer.

"Bob O'Ryan."

"And is Milly expecting you?"

"I think so. Her father probably told her I was going to drop by. I wanted to ask her some questions about the Hotline phone training."

"Okay, I've got to get back to my call. There's coffee in the urn, help yourself, and if Milly isn't finished soon, just wave at me and we can chat for a while and get to know each other a bit. I may even be able to answer some of your questions. That is, if I'm finished with my call. Okay?"

"Sure," I said, although Paula's machine-gun monologues had me wondering exactly what I was saying "okay" to. Boy, she sure was a non-stop talker. She also had made me feel completely welcome, and had quickly and efficiently found out my name, who I was looking for, and whether my business was urgent or not. Although she obviously was in the middle of a serious phone call, when she spoke to me, I had the feeling that Paula was giving me 100 percent of her attention. The whole exchange had taken less than a minute!

* * *

On the walls around the long table were posted lists of local phone numbers of various social service agencies, police and fire departments, and hospital emergency rooms, as well as 800 numbers for drug and alcohol information, and for reporting domestic violence and child abuse. The place was well-ordered chaos, like a beehive. Everyone seemed to know how to get their job done without getting in anyone else's way.

Along with the lists of phone numbers there were a few more sayings stuck on the walls. One said: "S— t happens to *everyone*. It's not what happens to you, it's what you do with it." Another said: "Listen. Reflect. Support. Don't be judgmental or tell people what to do. Your job is to <u>be there</u> for whoever is calling."

Phones kept ringing. I looked over at where Milly was sitting. I thought I would have recognized her even if Paula had not pointed her out. She had JD's green eyes, high cheekbones and strong jawline. She had glanced at the note Paula had written and had looked up and nodded in my direction, but since then had been huddled over the phone.

As she finally hung up, she called out, "Hi, Mr. O'Ryan. I'll be right with you." She spent the next couple of minutes writing in a ledger next to her and then came around the table and shook hands.

"You can call me Bob," I said. Milly seemed to be a serious young lady. I remembered JD had told me she was studying for her doctorate in a new branch of mathematics called "Chaos Theory."

"I hope you had no trouble finding this place," she said. "I couldn't get off that call any quicker. It was a call on the green phone— that's the 'suicide line'— and there's no way I could interrupt that. I've spoken to this particular woman before and she's often quite depressed.

"I have to have my 'antenna' completely extended every second to pick up whether she is really contemplating killing herself or not. If I think she is, I have to keep her on the line while I have someone else call the police and order an ambulance dispatched. Otherwise, my job is to talk her through it until she can calm down enough to wait and see her therapist or social worker the next day."

"What do you do, try and joke her out of her depression?" I said, with a nervous laugh.

"Oh no, that wouldn't be appropriate. Even if you or I think that someone else's troubles are trivial or silly, *they* are overwhelmed by them. They need to know that someone else cares, and is listening and hearing what their problems are... not trying to make light of them."

"Yeah, I guess that's true. But don't they say that if someone threatens that they're going to kill themselves, they really aren't serious about it?"

"Many people believe that, but it's not so. Often, the phone call they make to us is a real last call for help. It's a serious responsibility. And it gives you renewed respect for the phone." Her shoulders straightened slightly as she said this.

"How do you know which course of action to take?"

"We have to listen very carefully and assess the situation with specific 'probing' questions to determine just what stage the caller.is at. Part of our advanced training here is called 'Listening with the Third Ear.' That's where we learn to listen to the words behind the words someone is saying to us."

"*The words behind the words...* I like that."

"Every message has many levels of meaning. We have to train ourselves to pick up as many of those communications as possible, both conscious or unconscious. Some of our senior staff members, after a few minutes on the phone, can know, without being told, if a caller is seated, standing, or lying down!"

"I cannot control what others say to me over the phone. I can control what I do with that–how I react."

"That sounds hard to believe, but I'm at the point where I'm trying to be open to anything. I don't know if your father told you, but I'm on the path of *telephone enlightenment* and I'm interested in any tricks or techniques I can pick up that will sharpen my phone skills."

"I'll be glad to tell you whatever I've learned, but remember what the great ballet dancer Nureyev said."

Of course, Nureyev was a dancer! And he should know about both inspiration and technique, I thought to myself. At that moment, one of the phones rang, and Milly excused herself to answer it, promising to return as soon as she could, and suggesting that I feel free to wander around. I sat down in a large overstuffed chair near to where Paula was on the phone. As I listened to her end of the conversation, the same one she had been having when I came in, I was astonished at how quiet and receptive the seemingly garrulous Paula had become.

Holding the phone attentively to her ear, with her eyes closed, the only words Paula murmured were an occasional "Um," "Uh-huh," or "Yeah, so then what...?" The tone of her voice had changed, too. It was almost like a mother telling a bedtime story. I thought I was a pretty good judge of character, and I had had her pegged as someone whose "talk switch" was stuck in a permanent "on" position.

Milly was still on the phone when Paula finally ended her call. She came over and sat down next to me. "It sure is busy right now. That was a 15-year-old who can't talk to his parents about their drinking. He's been threatening to leave home...

"We're having a flurry. Happens every full moon. How're you making out, Bob? Did you have a chance to talk to Milly? Did you get some coffee? Oh yes, I see you have a cup. So, what brings you here? Oh, wait a minute while I get myself a cup of tea and then— if the phone doesn't ring again, we can chat." She rolled her eyes skyward and got up to get some tea.

I was right, this woman really was a motormouth!

I walked behind her. "I'm studying how to use the phone more efficiently, and Milly's father had suggested that I ask Milly for some of the Hotline's *phone secrets.*"

Milly laughed. "There are no secrets here. At least not about how to use the phone to the best of your ability. We're offering our crisis hotline training in two months... if you want to sign up, that would be great. We're always looking for volunteers. You'll have a wonderful time, as well as learning a lot of our... special skills and being able to help lots of people."

Learning new skills and being able to help people sounded intriguing, but really, counseling potentially suicidal people and teenagers threatening to become runaways didn't seem to be my idea of having a wonderful time."Uh, I don't know. I'll have to think about it. But I do have a question for you..." As I fumbled for the right wording I began to feel my old lack of confidence for a moment.

She turned and looked at me. "Well, go ahead. Either I can answer it or I can't but I won't know until you ask." We both laughed.

"It's just that you're so talkative in person and when I was listening to you on the phone with Jason you weren't saying much at all."

"You're right about that, I do like to talk. Just comes natural to me. And I had to learn how and when that was appropriate. See that?" she said, pointing to the cover of her notebook. On the cover was a hand-drawn triangle.

"That's the LAF triangle. It's one of the things we learn in our training."

"The laugh triangle?"

"No, L.A.F.— it's initials. Stands for Love, Appropriateness, and Flexibility. Whatever my strategy is on the phone here, underlying it is the love for, or caring about the person on the other end of the phone. Secondly, certain types of behavior are just not appropriate for certain situations. If Jason there needed to 'vent', he wants me to listen, not be taking up all the airwaves with my stuff. Thirdly, I have to remind myself to be flexible enough to adapt. If something I'm doing is not working, change it!"

"So, how do you change from being such a..." I said, stopping in mid-sentence.

"Motormouth?"

I blushed. Had she read my mind? But Paula was laughing. "It's easy. I have a little phrase I repeat in my mind—you might have heard me say it before. It's based on my nickname. I say 'Easy, PZ.' Everytime I open my mouth when I'm on shift here, I say to myself, 'Easy PZ.' Then, if what I'm about to say is appropriate, I 'floor it.' If not, I store it. And, of course, keep listening. Most people who call here don't really want to hear about me, they want to tell me about themselves."

"But, if you're not saying anything, don't they think you're not listening?"

"Oh, no. Not at all. In fact, saying nothing can often communicate acceptance, which is what these folks are not getting at home. That feeling of being accepted can, in turn, encourage them to take a more realistic look at how they can constructively grow and change. On the other hand, we sometimes get callers who are so shy and reticent, that we are trained to go into an *active listening* mode, which takes a much more involved role in the dialog."

Paula— or should I say PZ— pulled a printed sheet from a drawer and handed it to me. There was a short list on it:

> 1) *Pay attention to what the other person has to say.*
> 2) *Have empathy and rapport to help the person with his/her problem. Tomorrow it may be yours.*
> 3) *Consider as sacred the other person's feelings and view of the universe. What is real to them is real to them. You have to deal with that even if it may appear illogical.*
> 4) *Assume that every person has all the resources for change. Assume, whether true or not, that they are not broken and need to be fixed. Let the person arrive at a new option on their own, and acknowledge it. This empowers them.*
> 5) *What we see, hear, and feel are only approximations of reality. In a certain sense they are all inaccurate and transitory in nature. Be patient, they will change.*
> 6) *Every person has their story, their myth. Scratch the surface and you'll find a thriller in the most ordinary person.*

"We base a lot of our phone artistry on the approach of Carl Rogers," PZ continued. "He said the three most important attributes in any kind of communication are empathy, genuineness, and unconditional positive regard."

"Saying very little or nothing at all can sometimes be just what I need to do to communicate most powerfully during a phone conversation."

So JD wasn't the only one who thought of the ability to use the phone well as being an art form. I remembered JD also had a quote by Carl Rogers on his wall on the power of listening. PZ was still delivering information a mile a minute.

"Although specific phone skills can be taught, really effective communication on the phone requires creativity and inspiration."

"Well, that's easy for you to say, but how can I be creative and inspired when I start to freeze up on the phone? Sometimes I get worried I won't be able to say the right thing."

"Okay, first of all, you've got to trust yourself. You're a lot wiser than you give yourself credit for. As soon as you begin to trust yourself more, you'll pay attention to the little creative voice inside, which always knows just the right thing to say. If there is such a thing. I prefer to think that there are lots of right things. And second of all, if you want to be inspired, breathe."

"Breathe?"

"Yes. Before you speak, while you are listening, or even before answering the phone, take a few deep, purposeful breaths. It not only calms you, it will also slightly lower your voice timbre. Did you know the word 'inspiration' originally meant to breathe in?"

* * *

While I was pondering this last little revelation, the phone rang again. PZ squeezed my hand, excused herself and went to answer it. I looked over and saw Milly. She was finished with her call and motioned for me to join her.

"So, I see you were talking to PZ— or should I say listening to her?"

"Yes. She's quite an amazing person. You know, your dad is also quite a guy. He has really helped me a lot."

Milly smiled and didn't say anything.

"He said I should ask you who the *most real phoney* here was, so I could get some pointers from him."

Milly giggled. I could tell she recognized one of her father's word plays. "Mr. O'Ryan, you don't have to look any further. Either by accident, or synchronicity, you've already found that person. And it's not a him, it's a her. You've heard the expression 'Born with a silver spoon in your mouth?' Well, we say PZ was 'born with a silver phone in her ear.' If you wanted to learn the 'insider's view' of the telephone, you just interviewed the right person!"

* * *

O'RYAN'S PHONEMASTERY NOTES:

1) Techniques are necessary, but there is no substitute for inspiration. Trust yourself.

2) When you have to put someone on hold, let them know for how long. If it turns out to be longer, let them know. People on hold don't feel so much in limbo if they have a time frame.

3) Even if your time is very limited, give the other person 100 percent of your attention while you are on the phone with them. Most "rush and hurry" situations are self-created and can be changed more easily than we realize.

4) Learn to listen to *the words behind the words.* Imagine yourself having an antenna you can extend to pick up what is being communicated, but not necessarily

verbalized. Communication is multi-leveled. **Learn to listen with the third ear.**

5) Remember the LAF triangle: Love, Appropriateness and Flexibility. The person on the other end will sense if you genuinely care about them. Be aware of when your behavior or reaction is appropriate. If it's not, be flexible enough to adapt, according to which strategy will produce the best results. **If you also do what you've always done, you'll always get what you've always gotten.**

6) Sometimes saying very little, or not saying anything at all, is a powerful communication tool. Silence can be rich and warm, as well as cold and distant.

7) **Remember to breathe.**

CHAPTER FIVE

PHONES HAVE FEELINGS, TOO!

Befriending The Phone

Two weeks had passed since my visit to the Hotline. Between JD's lists of the types of phoners, and Milly and PZ's advice on listening skills, I felt like I was coming a lot closer to understanding the magic of the telephone. When I made calls from work, most of the time I was having more fun on the phone, and I was starting to sell more policies.

I thought I'd try to call JD and give him a progress report. I reached for the phone and dialed, without even giving myself time for a second thought. After two rings a voice answered "John Deltone here."

I was very surprised. "JD, hello. This is Bob O'Ryan. I didn't expect you to answer your own phone. I thought Martha always did that."

"Martha's on her lunch break and, if I'm not tied up with something, why shouldn't I answer the phone? After all, it might be an important call, like yours, that I wouldn't want to miss." I had a sudden picture of JD smiling—by George, he was right. He had told me you could "hear" someone smile on the phone, and I just had!

"So, Bob, how are you?"

"Well, it's been quite an interesting few weeks, to say the least!"

"To say the *very* least!"

"I've come a long way thanks to you. But I still have a couple of glitches."

"Such as?"

"First of all, even though I understand, on a mental level, everything you told me about the telephone being a powerful and magical tool, and not to be intimidated by it, I still have flashes of my old fears and hesitation about using it. I feel like I'm backsliding."

"That's pretty normal. What else?"

"I'm not quite sure how to put this, but it seems like there are too many miscommunications. I mean, even after I reach my customers, and I think we've agreed on something, they often have an entirely different idea of what the deal was. It's frustrating."

"Bob, I think it's time for you to check out Dr. Randolf's seminar. Jerry Randolf is an old friend of mine. In fact we used to be in the same fraternity at college. When I went into satellite interfaces, he went into teaching communication techniques. He's on the list I gave you, and I think he might have the answers to some of your questions. In fact, Jerry is giving an evening intensive this Friday. Want me to call him up and see if I can get you in as my guest?"

I quickly checked my appointment book. "That sounds terrific, and I'm free Friday. But, if you're too busy, I'll be glad to call Dr. Randolf."

"I'm glad to see some of your old reticence about using the phone is evaporating. But let me make this call, it will give me the opportunity to chat with Jerry. We have some catching up to do. I'll call you later with the details."

* * *

"If my behavior or reaction is not appropriate, I must be flexible enough to change it, according to which phone strategy will produce the best results."

True to his word, JD did call me back, and he had arranged for me to be his guest at the seminar. In addition, he suggested that the following weekend I accompany him on a business trip to Washington, D.C., where I would be able to meet the next person on his list, a Dr. Eugene Ferraro.

That Friday, I found myself in the lobby of a plush hotel in the midtown area of town. Above the entrance to one of the conference rooms was a hand-lettered sign that said **Befriending The Phone**. After filling out a form and getting a name tag, I entered and seated myself toward the front of the room. The rest of the audience was composed of about 40 to 50 well-dressed men and women of all different age groups and lifestyles.

On the small stage at the front of the room was a rather curious sight. In the middle was a speaker's podium with a heavy, black, old-fashioned phone sitting on top of it. Behind this was a large blackboard. On one side was a long low table with about two dozen telephones; on the other side was a chair, and one 6-foot-high phone of inflated plastic.

In front and off to one side of the stage a short bald man with a moustache was engaged in what looked like an animated discussion with a couple of young executive types in three-piece suits. He glanced at his watch, said a few more words and jumped up to the stage, clapping his hands.

"Hi. I'm Jerry Randolph. Please call me Jerry. I can't wait to get started; we're going to have some fun." He turned and walked to the blackboard and wrote: "There are 56 telephones per 100 people in the U.S. Washington, D.C. has 130 phones per 100 people. Americans make 188 billion calls per year. And sometimes I think my fourteen-year-old daughter makes half of them."

The audience laughed.

"And these statistics," he continued, with a grin, "are a couple of years old. Things in the telecommunications industry are moving so fast I haven't been able to get newer stats. Anyway, one thing is obvious, we are a society that has become heavily dependent on the telephone. Everybody's got one— at least one— and everyone needs to know how to use their phone to the best of their ability. Tonight we're here to learn about communication techniques as applied specifically to the telephone. First, let me ask you a couple of questions." His penetrating glance swept the audience.

"When your phone rings, what is the first thought or feeling that you have? When you have to make a call, do you look forward to it with gleeful anticipation, or is the thought of it so unpleasant that you think up a million reasons to put it off?"

I could feel my face flush. Had JD told him all about me? Suddenly I realized that a number of other people in the audience were shifting in their seats, and there was a scattering of nervous laughter. Of course I wasn't alone in my phone anxieties! Everybody in this room was here because they were less than 100 percent satisfied with their telephone skills.

"There are simple and powerful ways to re-orient, or reframe your negative feelings towards the phone into positive ones. And we'll get to a number of those." He paused, then said, "I'd like a volunteer, please."

A slender young woman in the first row raised her hand.

"Yes Renee," he said, squinting slightly to make out the name on the name-tag, "come right up here, if you would."

As Renee climbed up the stairs on the side of the

stage, Jerry reached behind the podium. He must have thrown a switch, because the next thing that happened, one of the phones— the one sitting on top of the podium— began to ring. Renee looked a little startled.

Jerry turned and broadly winked toward the audience. "Renee, would you get that, please?"

As Renee hesitated, Jerry said to the rest of us, "Watch and listen carefully."

The phone kept ringing. Renee's shoulders seemed to tighten and pull in toward her body. Her nose wrinkled as if she smelled something distasteful. She finally walked over to the ringing phone, picked it up and said "Hello?" with a decided rise in inflection.

Jerry picked up one of the other phones on the table and said, "Hi Renee, it's me, Jerry Randolph. How are you tonight?"

"Oh, I guess I'm okay, although I'm a little bit nervous up here."

"You're okay *and* a little bit nervous on stage? All right Renee, why don't you sit down? Maybe that would help you feel less nervous."

As she sat, she crossed her legs and held the elbow of her right arm with her left hand. Her head and shoulders were hunched forward.

"Are you ready, Renee?"

"Yes, Dr. Randolph."

"I wonder if you would tell me why you came to the seminar tonight. And please call me Jerry."

"I'm not comfortable on the phone, Jerry. I'm *always* scared to talk to people on the telephone. I hope I can learn to handle phone calls better."

"Uh huh. You're here because you hope to learn better ways of handling phone calls. Up to this moment in time you've been scared to talk to people on the phone because you're uncomfortable. You have never ever been comfortable on the phone. Not even *once* in your whole life?"

"Well, I exaggerated. I'm comfortable with my husband and other members of my family. Certain friends too, come to think of it."

"So, it's just certain types of phone calls to certain types of people that create problems for you."

"Right!" A smile blossomed on her face.

"That's *a long way* from being always scared and uncomfortable, don't you think?"

"Yes, it is, now that you mention it. I feel better already"

"Fine, you graduate and class is dismissed!" When the class stopped laughing and clapping, Jerry asked, "What kind of work do you do, Renee?"

"Well, I run a daycare center for pre-school kids... I love kids, and I'm real good with them. But when the parents call, I can't talk to them on the phone."

"You can't talk to them about anything?"

"I have no problem describing the activities at the school, or how I work with the kids."

"What is it that you can't talk to them about?"

"It's really finances. When they ask how much it costs, or when tuition needs to be paid... I just get all... tongue-tied. If they come in and I get a feel for them it's easier. But over the phone I just can't talk money. It feels too heavy."

I already had Renee pegged for a kinesthetic, based on what I had learned from JD. She spoke slowly, in a low voice, there were long pauses in between words, and a couple of deep sighs. Also, phrases like "tongue-tied" and "get a feel for" were right off my list. I was curious to see what Jerry Randolph would do.

"So, you would like to get a handle on how to talk to grown-ups on the phone about money? I bet you'd like some concrete information, so you could unravel this problem."

Ah-hah. I was right. Jerry had picked right up on Renee being a kinesthetic and was **speaking back to her in the same language.**

Renee uncrossed her legs, sat up straighter, and her face brightened.

"Yes, that's it, exactly. I've told myself that the next time I have to deal with this, I'm really going to try to do better, but each time is the same as before."

"Okay, thank you so much Renee. It's been a pleasure talking with you on the phone, and I hope I can help you come to grips with this and together we can come up with some constructive and creative solutions."

"Thanks, Dr. Randolph." She hung up the phone and left the stage.

"Okay, phone cadets, tell me what you noticed. Stanley?" He looked over to where a man in a turtleneck sweater had his hand raised.

"Renee made a funny face when she had to answer the phone."

"Yes, she didn't look too happy about that, did she? Anything else?"

"I noticed at the beginning of the conversation you repeated Renee's sentences back to her almost word for word."

"Absolutely right, Stanley. That's called 'mirroring.' If anyone here has ever had any phone counseling training, that's usually one of the first things you learn. There's nothing that can put someone more at ease, and make them feel like you understand them better, than to hear their own words repeated back to them. What I was doing is also called 'establishing rapport.' Anything else?"

A woman sitting next to me called out, "Her whole body looked like it was very tense. Like she was tied up in knots when she was talking to you at first. Then it gradually relaxed."

"Very good, Lucy," Jerry beamed. "You folks are pretty sharp. There are several ways to check your mood while on the phone. One way is to have the phone positioned near to a mirror. As you talk on the phone, watch yourself. Watch your face—what do the expressions on your face tell you about your mood. How much of those feelings come through nonverbally to the person at the other end?"

"Also, watch your posture. Do you shift posture? If so, at which moments? When did Renee shift posture?"

I raised my hand. "When you matched her representational system?"

Jerry Randolph shot me a quick, penetrating glance. "Oh, you're Bob O'Ryan, JD's friend. I should have known he'd send a *ringer* to my phone seminar," he said, raising his eyebrows like Groucho Marx.

"You're absolutely right, Bob. I'm not sure we'll have time to go into representational systems tonight, so if any of you folks want to know what we're talking about, go talk to Bob during the break."

I gulped. This was going a little quickly for me. I had become an overnight expert.

"Now Renee," he said, taking his attention off me, "when you look in the mirror, and catch yourself frowning while you're on the phone, try an experiment. Change your emotional state by rearranging your facial muscles. Much to your amazement, your emotions will follow suit. A smile transmits nerve impulses from facial muscles to the brain's emotional center, the lymbic system. By

I wondered what he meant by that. I hadn't noticed Renee swearing.

Jerry turned to the blackboard behind the podium and wrote: **The Five Linguistic Helpers.**

"'The structure of our language affects the functioning of our nervous systems.' A guy named Alfred Korzybski said that. Think about it. We know that how we feel affects our posture and facial expression. We just learned that it works the other way, too. Well, guess what? It's true for language, as well. We all know that how we think affects how we speak. At least I think we all know that. Many of us may not be quite as aware that how we speak affects how we think, feel, and act."

Underneath the heading, while he was speaking, Jerry had written:

1. Put all presenting problems and negative self descriptions in the past tense.

2. Change "but" to "and."

3. Change "can't" to "won't."

4. Change "should" to "could."

5. Eliminate the use of the word "try."

"Does anybody remember what Renee said when I asked her why she came to the seminar?"

An older black woman raised her hand, and said "She told you she was scared to talk on the phone. That she wasn't comfortable on the phone."

"Good listening, Marianne. Now, what happened to Renee when I applied the first helper and questioned her generality of *always* ?"

"She brightened up and her body posture became more confident."

"Right. When Renee gets in the habit of saying 'I *used* to be scared to talk on the phone, *in the past*,' or '*up until this moment in time* , I haven't been comfortable on the phone,' all of a sudden she's freed up the present and the future for new and delightful behaviors and skills. She's no longer bound by her past behavior. At any moment, she can make a radical change in her behavior, because linguistically, she already has done so!"

"Okay, on to the second helper: Change 'but' to 'and.'"

He went over to the table and picked up one of the phones there. He carried it down into the audience, walked over to where I was sitting and handed it to me. "Bob, let's pretend you're calling me up. You're a... let's say a graphic designer, and I'm an art director. Your call has two purposes. First, you just sent some work in and you're calling to see if I liked it. Second, you haven't met me in person, and you want to set up an appointment to come to my agency. Okay?"

"Okay." I took the phone, thought of what I had just learned and took a deep breath and let it out. I became aware of the tension in my shoulders and neck and let my head drop and rolled it from side to side. By the time Jerry walked back up on stage and answered one of the other phones (which he had set ringing by pushing the same button as before), I felt a warm glow in my stomach instead of the cold knot I often used to get when I had to use the phone.

"Hello. Jerry Randolph here."

"Oh hi, Jerry, this is Bob O'Ryan. I was calling to see if you had a chance to look at those sketches I sent over."

"Bob, I did look at them. You have a clever mind. They're quite... interesting. Very innovative. But they're not really what our agency is looking for now."

"Oh, that's too bad." Even though I was playing an imaginary character I still felt a bit crestfallen and rejected. "Uh, Jerry, I thought I might be able to come to your offices and meet with you later this week. I have a bunch of ideas that I'd like to show you."

"I'd love to Bob, but I'm really busy this week."

"Well, okay. Why don't you call me when you're free."

"Okay, Bob. In fact, let's have lunch some day. Take care, and thanks for the sketches. I'll send them back to you later this week. Bye."

"So long."

Everyone applauded. I felt pretty good about my performance on the phone— in front of 50 people, no less. And I had a strong hint about what Jerry was getting at with his change 'but' to 'and' tool.

"Now, by telling Bob that I liked his work but that it wasn't what my agency was looking for now, what was the net result?"

Lucy said "I think Bob got the feeling that the 'but' negated what had come before."

"Absolutely right. Give Lucy a gold star. Whenever someone wants to deliver an unpleasant message on the telephone, they're likely to sugarcoat it first, then hit the 'But Button.' 'But' makes you feel schizophrenic, it splits things apart. 'And' is a connective.

"Now, if I had said to Bob 'I loved your work. It's terrific, and it's not what we're really looking for right now,' that would have been a whole different ballgame. That would have left the door open for the next sentence. Maybe 'I'd like to hold on to them. We may be able to use them on our next project' or something like that."

Stanley had his hand raised. "And it was the same thing setting up a meeting. When you told Bob you'd love to, but you were really busy this week."

"Okay, now if I had said 'Bob, I'd love to meet with you and this is a very busy week,' again, that points linguistically toward a following statement, like 'How about next week.' Instead of the real meaning of the first statement, which is, I really wouldn't love to meet with you, I'm just using a polite business formula."

Stanley was laughing, "I know that old 'let's have lunch some day' line. What that really translates to is 'End of conversation. I hope I never bump into you, even by accident.'"

Jerry laughed too. "You got that one right. Now, if you'll look inside the manila envelopes you each got at the beginning of the evening, you'll find a reprint of a very interesting article from the *N.Y. Times* of September 5, 1987, called 'I Don't Want to Criticize the Teaching of English, but...' by Thomas R. Trowbridge. If you read this, you'll see that there are many such phrases that have gotten secondary, pejorative meanings in contemporary conversation.

"So, just to summarize— those of you who have push button phones— remember, use the **But Button** sparingly.

"Okay, any questions? Good, on to the next helper: 'change can't to won't.' This is one that Renee used. Who's got a good memory? Marianne again?"

"She said, 'when parents call I can't talk to them on the phone.'"

"Marianne, do you have a tape recorder?"

"Sort of. I mean I've always been able to sort of replay back things I've heard people say in my mind. Almost as if I had a tape recorder in my head."

"That's a wonderful talent! I want to speak to you later, and see if I can model what you do. Maybe I can learn it. Sure would come in handy in my profession.

Anyway, when Renee said 'I can't talk to them' what did that mean? She *does* talk to them on the phone. Let's try substituting 'won't.' The sentence then becomes 'when parents call, I won't— or prefer not to— talk to them on the phone about money.'

"'Won't' is an empowering word. 'Can't' means you are unable. You have no choice. No say in the matter. 'Won't' means I can, but for some reason, which I don't yet understand, I choose not to." Jerry glanced over at Renee. "Is any of this making sense to you?"

Renee nodded slowly.

"I have a hunch Renee, that if you thought of the parents on the other end of the phone as needing your attention and love as much as the babies and children that you take care of, you'd start to feel differently about the phone, regardless of what you were talking about."

"We were on number four, 'change *should* to *could.*' Okay, more of the same. Neither Renee or Bob used 'the little dictator'— that's what I like to call 'should.' 'Should' tells you you must do this, you must do that, if you don't, you're a bad person and you have to feel guilty. Saying should is self-imposed stress. Think about it. There are very few shoulds. You're adults now, you decide on your personal commandments and musts. 'Could,' on the other hand, is another empowering word. It gives options, choices, and puts you back in command of your own ship.

"You don't always have to answer the phone! Think about that. Every time the phone rings, you can say to yourself, 'I could answer the phone.' Or how about returning calls? Instead of saying 'I should return so-and-so's call, you can say, 'I could return their call.' It gives you freedom of choice."

As I listened to Jerry speak, I was mentally reviewing my own choice of language. I often thought of things

I 'should' do. This was powerful information; I couldn't wait to see how some of my new insights could help my phone skills.

"Okay, last *and* not least..." Jerry said, with an emphasis on 'and', "eliminate the use of the word 'try.' Let's get a fresh volunteer. Arthur, would you come up here?"

A very young man, perhaps a college student, walked up to the front. Jerry reached behind the podium to push the button, and the phone began to ring again. "Arthur, would you try to answer that phone?"

Arthur hopped up on the stage, reached over and picked up the receiver. As he began to lift it up toward his ear, Jerry said "No, no, Arthur, you're answering it. I asked if you would *try* to answer it."

Arthur laughed and walked back to his seat. Jerry turned to us and said, "'Try' is a smokescreen word. As long as you are trying to do something, you're not doing it. Every time you promise someone you will try to do something, you're not making a commitment to do it.

"If an American businessperson negotiating with Japanese companies says he will 'try' to deliver an order on a particular date, the Japanese translation is 'it will not be delivered by that date.' It either will be or it will not. Try doesn't count.

"What did Renee say? She said she was 'really going to *try* to do better.' Do you understand? You're leaving the backdoor open so you can say, 'Well, I tried, but it just didn't work,' or 'it just didn't happen.'"

* * *

"Okay. That covers the Five Linguistic Helpers. I think we should try to take a break now." Everyone laughed. Jerry said, "See, we tried, but we didn't take one did we? We have so much to cover, how about a one-minute stretch? Everybody stand up." We all stood.

"Okay, now raise up on your tip-toes. Put your hands in the air and reach for the sky. That's it, stretch as high up as you can. Hold it for a count of ten, and let your hands slowly float down. Come down onto the soles of your feet. Now let your knees bend just slightly. Let your hands dangle freely at your sides. Close your eyes and picture your favorite color. Good. Take a deep breath and let it out. Another one, even deeper, and let it out. Now a third. And exhale. All right, you can sit again."

I felt great, as if I had just taken a hot shower or something. I couldn't figure it out. This guy was a magician. Jerry had turned to the blackboard and was energetically writing again. This time he had two headings. One said **Nominalization** and the other said **Concrete**.

Under the first he had written "abstract," "vague," "produces hallucinations," "unspecified," and "produces Transderivational Search (search for meaning)." Under the second word, Concrete, was written "specific," "definite," and "fits in a wheelbarrow."

"All language is broken up into two categories. All words, generally break down into one of two categories. Remember, these are *useful generalities*. Okay. I'm going to throw some words out and you tell me what they are. Now, if you want to find out if they're concrete words or nominalizations, ask yourself the question, 'Does it fit in a wheelbarrow?' If it fits in a wheelbarrow, it's generally a concrete word. Okay? Silk..."

"Concrete."

"Wood?"

"Concrete."

"Nails?"

"Concrete."

"Love?"

"Nominalization."

"Trust?"

"Nominalization."

"Patriotism?"

"Nominalization."

"Terrorism?"

"Nominalization."

"Car?"

"Concrete."

"Loyalty?"

"Nominalization."

"Friendship?"

"Nominalization."

"Very good. Now, the misuse of these words is the basis for all miscommunication between people. Suppose that Stanley and I are friends. One day I walk up to Stanley and I ask him, 'Stanley, can I borrow $10,000?' And he looks at me with complete innocence and says, 'But I thought you were my friend.' And I say, 'What do you mean? Of course we're friends. We've been friends for ten years.' And he says, 'Friends don't do that. They don't ask to borrow money. It ruins the friendship.' But that's because 'friendship' is a nominalization. In my world, that's what a friend can do.

"Okay, now a week later, Stanley calls me up at 3 o'clock in the morning. And I say, 'What! Who's this? What's going on here?' And he says, 'I need help. My mother just died. My father just lost his job. My wife left.' Whatever it is, it's a tragedy. And I say, 'But friends don't do this. 'Yeah, but I thought we were friends,' he says. 'Friends don't call you up in the middle of the night.'

Everybody has a different definition of 'friend.' You have to stop and ask, 'What do you mean, specifically? Who, specifically? Under what circumstances? When? How much?"

I was beginning to feel like when you've been working on putting together a jigsaw puzzle for a long time and suddenly you begin to see the picture that you're making. All the little pieces were beginning to fall into place. The miscommunications over the phone, the "sure deals" that went sour in my business, so many of the misunderstandings were due to the fact that my clients and I were using nominalizations for which we each had different definitions.

Jerry Randolph was still speaking. "... a Transderivational Search is an interior search through the pictures in your brain, which you pull forward in front of your own screen to make sense of what the other person is saying. So when they speak, for instance, you assume that they are talking about friendship in the same terms that you define friendship.

"We've got to develop skills to enable us to get precise information and to give precise information. We need to learn how to ask clarifying and qualifying questions. Now, if you'll just take a look inside your manila folders again, you'll find a very interesting little piece of paper. It's got an outline of a left hand on one side, and an outline of a right hand on the other. We call these our 'Phone Finger Tips'.

"You thought you were going to be able to just sit there and be passive all night? Nope. You're all going to be active participants in this next section of the seminar. Okay, begin by getting a partner; the person next to you or in front of or behind you. Everybody got one? Good.

"Now, move toward the walls and pillars. Each pair

RIGHT HAND

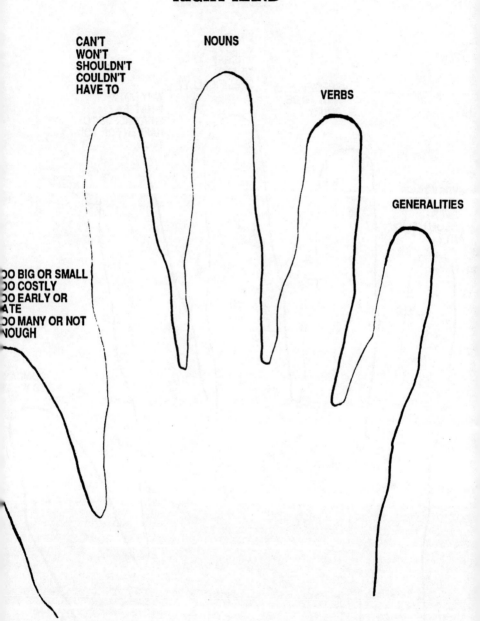

CAN'T
WON'T
SHOULDN'T
COULDN'T
HAVE TO

NOUNS

VERBS

GENERALITIES

OO BIG OR SMALL
OO COSTLY
OO EARLY OR
ATE
OO MANY OR NOT
NOUGH

LEFT HAND

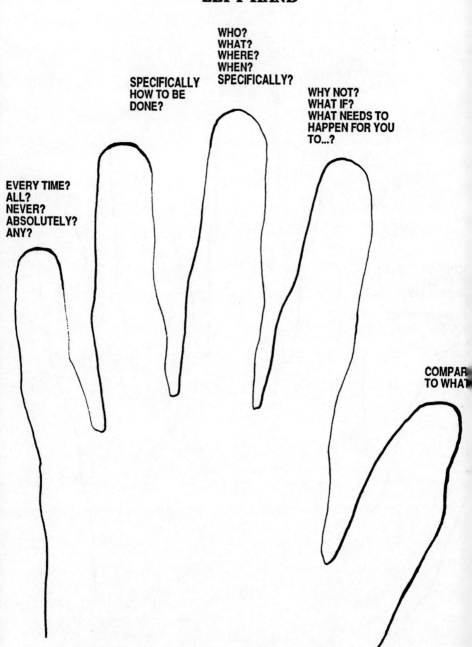

WHO?
WHAT?
WHERE?
WHEN?
SPECIFICALLY?

SPECIFICALLY
HOW TO BE
DONE?

WHY NOT?
WHAT IF?
WHAT NEEDS TO
HAPPEN FOR YOU
TO...?

EVERY TIME?
ALL?
NEVER?
ABSOLUTELY?
ANY?

COMPAR
TO WHAT

is going to have a 'receiver' and an 'operator.' First, I'd like the operator to place the right hand chart on the wall so it's about 6 inches above the receiver's head. Receiver, face the wall and put your right hand on the chart. Got that? Okay.

"Now operator, touch the receiver's thumb and read out loud what's written there... 'Too big or small, too costly, too early or late, too many or not enough.' Good. Say it over three or four times, as quickly as you can.

"Okay, now touch the receiver's index finger and read what's written there, 'Can't, won't, shouldn't, couldn't, have to.' The idea is to move quickly from one finger to another, repeating verbally what's written above each of the five fingers in the illustration. Receivers need not memorize or understand this, it's going in directly into your subconscious.

"When you've done that for about a minute, take down the right hand chart and put the left hand chart on the wall. Okay? Now receiver, put your left hand up against the chart. Got that? Good.

"Operator, do the same thing you did on the right hand with the left hand. Got it? Touch the pinkie and say, 'Everytime? All? Never? Absolutely? Any?'

"Next, touch the middle finger: 'Who, what, where, when— specifically?' Index finger: 'Why Not? What if? What Needs to Happen?' Do this with all five fingers on the chart. After you've done this for about a minute, take the chart down.

"Receivers put your hands together and take a minute to visualize yourself on the phone, using what you've just learned. When you've finished your visualization, switch. Operators become receivers and vice-versa. After you've finished this, we really will take a break."

* * *

creating facial muscle tension, a frown or grimace tends to induce anxiety.

"All of this is based on recent research. Psychologists have found that alterations in body configurations can bring about quick and powerful emotional changes. In other words there's a behavioral feedback loop. Many of you may already understand that your emotional state will influence your body. For example, if you're depressed, you're more likely to get sick.

"Body language will reflect— often unconsciously— your thoughts and emotions. What you may not realize is that the reverse is true. Put most simply, you can change the way you feel by changing your posture and facial expressions."

He walked over, picked up the telephone receiver and sat down. I noticed he was holding the phone so tight his knuckles were white.

His jaw was clenched, his brow furrowed, and his shoulders were up around his ears. He looked like he was hardly breathing.

"What's the difference between this... and this?" He leaned back, and his knuckles, jaw, brow, and shoulders relaxed. He also took a good deep breath and let it out.

"You just untied the knots," someone from the audience called out. "You relaxed."

"Absolutely correct. And don't you think the person at the other end of the phone can pick that up? You don't have to be psychic. It's frequently been pointed out by those who teach forms of relaxation that it is impossible to have an anxious mind in a relaxed body. Now, we want to learn not only to untie the knots in our muscles, but also the knots in our language. Which brings us to our next point. Let's see what we can do to clean up Renee's language."

During the break several people came over to me to ask about what I meant by representational systems. I found that, having to explain them to others, I already understood them far better than I thought I did. As people began to treat me as a sort of authority, I felt my confidence level rise 100 percent.

It wasn't til our short break was almost over that I was able to reflect briefly on what bearing the "Phone Finger Tips" drill and the information about *concrete words* and *nominalizations* could have on my rapidly developing arsenal of phone skills. Most of those "miscommunications" I had been experiencing recently with my clients at work were due to language that was too vague... to letting too many nominalizations, like "soon," or "too much," cloud my understanding.

During my next phone conversation, if someone said to me "I'll put that in the mail right away," I was going to say, "When, specifically?" Or if a prospective client told me that one of our policies was "too expensive," the phrase "Too expensive compared to what?" was ready to leap off my lips. Likewise, if I called home and Lisa asked why I had to work late every night, I was ready to lightly ask her "Every night... you mean there's never a night when I've been home early?" This was great stuff.

Jerry Randolph's voice broke through my reverie. "Okay, is everybody ready to let go of some more of their phone 'hang-ups'?"

A large groan from the audience greeted this remark.

Jerry was holding up a book. "We're going to talk about peak performance next— about states of excellence— and I would highly recommend this book to all of you who are interested in this subject. It's by Dr. Charles

"The foundation of my phone skills is how much I learn to trust myself."

Garfield, and it's called *Peak Performance: Mental Training Techniques of the World's Greatest Athletes.*

"Dr. Garfield speaks of attaining the state of letting go, of feeling like you were in a dream where everything goes right effortlessly. Some athletes have described this as 'playing in a trance,' or 'going on automatic pilot.' Business people call it 'being on a roll'— you're in the right place at the right time, your timing is impeccable, you make sales and close deals without even trying. Most people stumble onto these states of excellence by accident. We attribute it to our lucky stars..."

"Yeah, or our biorhythms," someone shouted out.

"Right. Well, here's some exciting news: you can teach yourself to go into states of excellence, peak performance states, at will. How many times have you heard someone say something like 'I wore that dress the day I met the man of my dreams. It's my good luck dress. Every time I wear it, something good happens.' What happens is..."

Jerry turned to the blackboard and wrote the words **Belief system, Behavioral Loop,** and **Anchor.** He turned back to us and continued, "What happens is you've constructed a behavioral loop to reinforce your belief system. You now believe so strongly that a certain dress is lucky, when you wear it, you are looking for good things to happen. You are *expecting* them to happen, and you are paying attention to them.

"So when they do— and some good things happen almost every day to almost everyone— you say to yourself, 'See, I knew it. It's a magical dress.' And the belief system grows stronger for the next use. Are all belief systems positive? Who can think of an example of a negative belief system?"

I raised my hand. "I always believed that if I didn't

get eight hours sleep, I would be miserable the next day...
I wouldn't be able to focus, or do anything right."
"Good. A lot of people believe that one. And, Bob,
what happens if you don't get eight hours sleep?"
"I'm usually in a pretty rotten mood the next day."
"Okay Bob, how many nominalizations in that
sentence?"
Everyone laughed. I was laughing, too. "Let's see.
I guess 'usually' is one, and 'pretty rotten' would be
another."
"How about a phone belief system? We've already
heard Renee's. Anyone else have one of those?"
Next to me, Lucy had her hand up. "I can't really
concentrate on the phone if someone else in the room is
talking."
"Now let me guess. You work in a busy office with
lots of other people in the room, right?"
"Of course. That's why I'm here."
"Thank you, Lucy. We'll send you out of here with
a new belief system. As long as you can prove it correct,
you'll be fine. See, the bottom line of all our meta-
programs is that the unconscious wants us to be right.
So, we seek experiences and interpret them to confirm
our beliefs."
He picked up a notebook, and read from it: "Ed-
ward E. Jones, a psychologist at Princeton University,
went one step further. He said, 'Our expectancies not only
affect how we see reality but also affect the reality itself.'
Consider the implications of that statement!"
"All right. Now, the big breakthrough was when
behavioral engineers began to realize that we can learn to
use an arbitrary signal or object to get ourselves into a
certain frame of mind. What's currently referred to as an
'altered state.' This object or signal is sometimes called an

'anchor.' So, who can guess what we call the use of this signal?"

"Anchoring?"

"Give that man a cigar. Nope, on second thought, we don't want to anchor getting the right answer with something that smells that bad. But before we get into anchoring, does anybody here have a positive belief system about the phone?"

Arthur said, "I recently got a cordless phone. And I'm so much more comfortable on the phone ever since I got it. I don't feel like I'm on a leash, connected to the wall."

"Good, Arthur, there's an example of an anchor. Your cordless phone is your anchor to feeling better on the phone—which leads to better phone skills. Anyone else with a positive phone belief system? Yes, Marianne?"

"Well, this sounds silly, but I have this superstition that if I pick up the phone before the second ring, it will be good news."

"Speaking of superstitions, all you sports fans out there must be familiar with anchoring... A baseball player, for instance, when he has gotten ten hits in a row with a particular bat, will call that bat his 'lucky bat.' The behavior of being a good hitter is then anchored to that bat. What's the only problem with that anchor? Bob?"

I found myself answering before I had time to think. "If the bat breaks, he loses his anchor?"

"That's correct." Jerry was pacing around the stage. This was obviously a subject near and dear to his heart. "Or how about Jimmy Connors, the tennis player. What does he do when he hits a winning shot? He anchors it with a clenched fist afterward. Smart man, the anchor is in a part of his body, in a gesture. It's not a 'lucky rabbit's foot' that he can lose.

"Though I may dis-agree with someone over the phone, I must respect their universe. Whatever their point of view, it is real to them."

"All right, we're going to do an exercise in anchoring our power state, especially to the telephone, for easy access to excellence in communication. First I'll demonstrate with a victim—I mean a volunteer..." Everyone laughed. "Stanley, would you come up here?"

Stanley came up and climbed up on stage next to Jerry. Jerry, in the meantime, had taken one of the phones from the table and placed it on a chair. "Stanley, I want you to choose a part of your body to touch, maybe someplace on your hand, or a word you can repeat, subvocally, in a social situation without being conspicuous. It may be something as simple as crossing your fingers, or putting your hand to your chin, or the word 'focus.' Use your imagination. Perhaps you already have such a gesture that you use to anchor good times.

"Okay, got one? Now imagine a circle around this chair and phone, about three feet in diameter. Can you see it?"

Stanley nodded, "Uh huh."

"Good. Now I'm going to ask you to picture a number of moments in your life when you had a peak experience."

"Stanley, close your eyes and picture a moment in your life of peak experience in humor. It could have been a time when you were incredibly funny, or perhaps something was so funny you thought you'd never stop laughing. Got one?"

Stanley had a big smile as he nodded.

"Now, step up to the phone, into the circle, and 'set' your anchor. This is done by making the gesture, or touching the part of the body, or repeating the word or phrase you have chosen to be your anchor. Then hold the phone and run a mental movie of that peak experience."

As he stepped into the imaginary circle, Stanley

pulled at his earlobe. I guess this was his 'anchor.' Then he reached over and picked up the phone. Standing there with his eyes closed, holding the phone, Stanley started to laugh at his memory.

"Good. Put the phone down, release your anchor, and step out of the circle. Now, picture a moment in your life of peak performance in sports. Got one? Okay, step into the circle, set your anchor, and hold the phone."

"Okay, picture a time in your life when you won some kind of an award, or achieved public recognition for your excellence." Stanley was shaking his head as if he were having trouble with this one until Jerry said "It could be something from your childhood, like winning your class spelling bee in 3rd grade, or something from your adult life."

Stanley nodded, stepped into the circle, set his anchor, and picked up the phone. This whole procedure was repeated several times for the categories of peak experiences in making love, in spirituality/nature, in business, on the phone, and in successfully overcoming an obstacle or challenge. When it was over I swear Stanley was visibly glowing.

"All right, now pair off. I'm going to give each pair one of our telephones and I want you to each go through this drill with your partner. When you're finished, switch, so that everybody gets a chance to anchor their state of excellence to the phone."

After we had all finished our drills, which took about ten minutes, Jerry asked for our attention. He was caressing the six-foot high cardboard phone on the side of the stage while he spoke.

"You have now transferred your most positive, powerful experiences of your life, and the feelings that go with them, to the telephone. You can repeat this a couple of times, if you'd like, when you get home tonight. Also, over the next couple of weeks, whenever you have a powerful or playful experience on the phone— and you'll be having a lot more of them, now— anchor it to your spot. It will become more and more powerful.

"You'll also find that when you have to make calls, especially business calls and you are just not in 'the mood,' you can simply fire off your anchor of excellence and begin dialing. By the time the call goes through, you will have entered that peak performance state you desire. This emergency power boost can last up to several hours, at which time you can reactivate it with the same procedure.

"And now, before we finish up for the evening, I just wanted to talk for a minute about finding the right phone. It's like finding the right car, or the right house... it's very important. Now me, for instance, I like big. I drive a Lincoln Continental, my wife is 6'1", and my phone...." he tapered off as he continued to fondle the very large mock phone in the front of the room. It was a rather unforgettable image.

"The more you work with a particular tool, the more you become familiar with it. The more familiar you are with it, the more proficient you become with it. It begins to be an extension of you, rather than something separate. You grow accustomed to the feel of the phone, the smell of it, the look and sound of it. Some people like the heavy weight of the old-fashioned type of phone. They are not accustomed to newer, light-weight models. There are phone stores where you can purchase the older style phones.

"If the ring of your phone throws you off, get a phone with a different ring. Novelty phones are available that buzz, chime, bark like a dog, or even play a familiar melody, like a music-box. Learn to play with the high-tech variety that's available to you. Or, as Mr. Natural would say, 'Use the right tool for the right job.'"

"It's been a pleasure. Good night everyone, and don't forget to make friends with your phone. Give it a name, imbue it with a likeable, cooperative disposition... a personality. Remember, phones are fun."

We all stood and gave Jerry Randolph a hearty round of applause. I felt like a transformed person as I left the hotel that night. I couldn't wait to get home and tell Sheryl what I was learning about the phone. And, by extension, about communication in general.

* * *

O'RYAN'S PHONEMASTERY NOTES:

1) Nonverbal information, postures and facial expressions are transmitted over the phone just like words.

2) There are several ways to check your mood while on the phone. One way is to have the phone positioned near a mirror. As you talk on the phone watch yourself.

3) Body language will reflect your thoughts and emotions. The reverse is also true. You can change the way you feel by changing your posture and facial expressions. For example a smile transmits nerve impulses from facial muscles to the brain's emotional center, the lymbic system. By creating facial muscle tension, a frown or grimace tends to induce anxiety.

4) To help empower our verbal communication:

    a) Put all presenting problems and negative self descriptions in the past tense.

    b) Change *but* to *and*.

    c) Change *can't* to *won't*.

d) Change *should* to *could.*

e) Eliminate the use of the word *try.*

5) All words are broken up into two categories, nominalizations and concrete words. The former is vague and produces miscommunications. Understanding the implications of the two categories is a powerful communication tool.

6) By asking clarifying and qualifying questions, you can take the fuzziness out of generalizations and nominalizations in phone conversation.

7) There is a state of excellence called Peak Performance. Athletes describe this as "playing in a trance," "going on automatic pilot," or the "White Moment." Business people call it "being on a roll." There are techniques now available that enable a person to enter that special state at will by use of "anchors."

8) Learn to use an arbitrary signal or object— an "anchor"— to get yourself into a state of excellence. You can anchor your state of excellence to the telephone!

CHAPTER SIX

THE HYP PHONIST

The weekend after Jerry Randolf's seminar I felt like I was flying. In fact I was flying. Being on the jet to Washington with JD certainly had a different feeling to it than the first time we flew together, when we met. We took turns making calls from the in-flight phone. I was really beginning to understand how to have fun with the phone.

JD refused to tell me anything about Dr. Ferrara except that he was a hypnotist.

"A what?" I said, in surprise and disbelief.

"A hypnotist," he said as if it were the most normal thing in the world.

The word "hypnotist" conjured up all sorts of strange images in my mind. I pictured a thin man with over-sized eyes (that had little spirals in them like the ones used on the old television show *Twilight Zone*), wearing a goatee and a menacing look. Memories of movies from the 1940's coursed through my brain— *Svengali, Trilby,* and later movies like *The Manchurian Candidate*, and *Telethon*.

In plain English, I was nervous.

To be perfectly honest, I was scared silly.

There was a light rain and the heavy smell of cherry blossoms in the air. His office was on St. Charles Street, an historical, beautiful, and expensive part of our nation's capitol. The cobblestone streets glimmered under the old street gas lamps. Everything looked fresh and magical. It was one of those extraordinary moments in one's life where time seems to stand still and everything holds promise of renewal and the unexpected.

And the unexpected was exactly what happened.

It wasn't more than two minutes after meeting Dr. Ferrara that I began to feel ridiculous, and all my misconceptions began to evaporate into thin air. I was warmly greeted by a pleasant, gray haired man in his late fifties pushing his way toward me in a wheelchair. The office was tastefully furnished with antique furniture, wall-to-wall books, a beautiful old roll-top desk with a Tiffany lamp that gave off a soothing, greenish glow.

"Well, Mr. O'Ryan, glad to meet you. I spoke to JD yesterday and he told me that you are quite a go-getter. I love enthusiasm. Did you know it means filled with God?"

"Really? That's very interesting. It's good to meet you, Doctor."

"Please," he said shaking his head, "just call me Gene."

"Okay, Gene."

"You look a little pale. Was your flight okay?"

"Yes, it was fine. I guess I'm just a little surprised."

"About what."

"Oh nothing really."

"I love it when people say, 'oh just nothing.' It usually translates into, 'this is really important.'"

"You got me there. I just expected someone different. You know, like in the movies."

Gene laughed and pointed to a picture on his wall. It was a page from some cheap magazine advertising

"I can eliminate fuzziness from my phone conversations by learning to be specific, and by asking others clarifying and qualifying questions."

hypnosis and it had one of those pictures of a hypnotist with intense penetrating eyes and some sort of "beam" emanating from them, like a grade B science fiction movie. "Like that?"

Now, I had to laugh. "You're right, that's sort of what I expected."

"That's okay, Bob, I'm used to it. Most people have that misconception. *Really there is no such thing as hypnosis*," he said in a conspiratorial tone.

"What?" I exclaimed. "But you are a famous hypnotist." I pointed around the room and said insistently, "You must have at least a thousand books here on hypnosis. Now I'm confused!"

"Good," he said enigmatically, "confusion is a very beneficial state."

"Now I'm *really* confused."

"You see, hypnosis is really just effective communication, with others or just with yourself."

"Then what is this trance state I hear so much about?"

"It is a natural state. In my lectures I always say that my job as a hypnotherapist is not to put people into a trance but to *get them out of the trance they are already in*. That is, if the trance they are in is not affording a person easy and effective access to their unlimited potentials and deep personal resources. I hear that you had been, for example, in a negative trance about the telephone. You had fears and apprehension and minimal effectiveness using that tool. Hasn't that changed for you?"

"Yes, an awful lot. I still have some things to learn."

"We all do," he said, rolling his chair closer to me. He looked like the perfect grandfather. He was wearing a three piece suit with the vest unbuttoned, tie untied, and a gold chain of a pocket watch dangling from the side. Below a full head of thin gray hair was a soft face with a wise-looking moustache; he had welcoming, fun-loving, sparkling eyes with just the tiniest glint of childish mischievousness, as if any moment he was about to spring out of his chair declaring that he had pulled off a wonderful prank.

He paused for a moment, and then continued, "Personal growth is a process not a product. As far as I know there is no time when we are perfect and finished learning. Anyway, to go back to your question, trance is something you do every day, you just don't use that word to describe it. It is a *natural* state. For example, day-dreaming, lying in bed in the morning not quite awake, driving long distances, or standing on line at the bank or supermarket are all natural trance states. How many times have you dialed a number and as the phone was ringing you went into a trance thinking about something else and couldn't remember who you called?"

"I never do that!" I joked. We both laughed.

"By the way, would you like a cup of coffee?" he asked.

"That would be great."

As Gene poured the coffee he continued, "One of the best examples is going to the movies. If it is a good movie that captures your attention, you'll forget where you are until it's over and the lights go on. You were entranced. When we say someone is charismatic or has a magnetic personality they usually are mesmerizing in their communication with other people, whether over the phone or face-to-face."

"Like JD and PZ," I added.

"I don't know PZ, but that's certainly true of John Deltone."

"I read an article in a business magazine on stress management during my flight here. It mentioned visualizations and relaxation techniques. Are those the same as self-hypnosis?"

"Yes, that special state that is simply achieved by relaxing all the muscles of your body is called by many names: visualizations, guided imagery, progressive relaxation, autogenic training, meditation, daydreaming, and even praying. In medical terms it's called an alpha/theta brain wave. It seems that while the mind is in that state you can program or deprogram your mind."

"You keep talking about the mind as if it's some kind of computer."

"Well in fact one current metaphor does refer to the mind/brain as a kind of bio-computer composed of past information in the form of mental image pictures called holograms."

"Holograms?"

"Do you have a MasterCard on you?"

"Yes, I think I do." I reached into my suit and took my card from my wallet handing it to Gene.

On it was a small, three-dimensional picture of an eagle. "That's a hologram," said Gene. "They are rather popular now, novelty stores are full of them. They're made with laser light. Unlike two-dimensional photos, you can cut up a holographic picture, put it back in front of a laser light and get the entire picture again because all the information of the picture is equally distributed throughout the hologram."

"That's amazing!"

"Sure is. It's been proposed that the human mind records what it is experiencing at all times, whether we are conscious or not, and stores the information. It's available for retrieval whenever we want to remember it.

When we play back the 'movie' it seems to have motion, or we can freeze-frame a single picture and look at that."

"Can you give me an example?"

"Sure. Get a picture in your mind of your wife."

"Got it."

"Now your bedroom."

"Okay."

"What's you favorite sport?"

"Golf."

"Good. Now get a picture of your last golf game and run the movie of you playing the first couple of holes."

I must have had a peculiar look on my face because he asked me what was happening. I answered, "I missed a two-foot put."

Dr. Ferrara laughed. "Why don't you choose a game where you excelled. It might be more pleasant to look at."

I did. After a few seconds my memory-movie began to roll.

"Good. Now remember the gym of your high school."

"Got it."

"Okay, now your first car."

That was easy, it was a Volkswagon bug.

"How about the favorite teacher you had in grammar school."

That took a little longer, but the picture of Mrs. Brandon appeared inside my head clear as day.

"You see," he said, "all your memories are there in three-dimensional form. An interesting thing about these mental holograms is that they contain primarily three kinds of information. Visual, auditory and kinesthetic."

"You mean like the three types of callers?"

"Exactly!"

"You record what you saw, heard, felt, smelled, and—if you were eating—what you tasted. When you remember something from the past and pay attention to the memory, it activates the information and you'll see what you saw, hear the sounds, and feel the sensations *as if* it were happening all over again at the present moment. **Attention** is the key."

"Why attention?"

"Good question." He stopped a moment and seemed lost in thought and then said, "Get a picture in front of your mind's eye of all your worst characteristics. Everything negative you've thought about yourself or other people have said about you."

"You mean like I'm too skinny, lazy, bad on the phone. That sort of thing?"

"Right."

"Oh, boy," I said. It took about ten seconds but sure enough there I was in all my negative anti-glory. Standing paralyzed in front of the phone, frozen by apprehension of making a call, looking distraught, disorganized, lazy, stupid, ugly, unsuccessful... need I say more?

"Got it? Good. Put that picture over on the left side of your screen and now what I want you to do is make a composite of all the positive traits you have. Everything good you've ever thought about yourself, how you looked when you felt most powerful in your life, the best compliments people ever made to you, perhaps even a time when you made a good sale over the phone."

"All right." I knew this one was going to be easier and it was. "Okay, I have it."

"Fine. You're doing just fine. Now get the first picture of your negative aspects and bring it back on screen and put it next to the one you just made of all your wonderful characteristics. Like you had two separate slides on a screen."

Sure enough, there they were, plain as day.

"Okay, Bob, now I want to ask you a very important question. Which one of those pictures is true?"

I got a little nervous thinking this might be a trick question.

Gene's sensory acuity must have picked up my hesitation and he added, "just take a guess."

"Well," I answered, "to be perfectly honest with you, the one on the left."

"That's what I thought. Your self-love, self-trust level is low."

I was only trying to be honest. "That's the way I feel most of the time."

"I'm sure you do, at least that's the way you *used* to feel. You'll find, much to your own delight," he said in a lower tone of voice that made the words seem to hang in the air, "**that over the next hours, days, weeks, and months ahead, you begin to notice that you are loving yourself more, trusting yourself more, using the phone more powerfully with great ease and surprising success.**"

I don't know exactly what he did, but in the warm, comfortable silence that followed, the room seemed to change, and I had that odd sensation one gets now and again of time standing still. When he spoke his voice seemed very far away.

"So, Bob, which of those two pictures of you are true?"

"Oh, yes, I almost forgot. Let's say the positive one."

"Not really."

Now I was really confused. "The negative one?"

"No, not that either."

I thought for a moment longer. "Both?"

"Right!" he said, ringing a little brass bell on his desk. "Both pictures are true and not true. It depends on the one you choose to be true, *the one you pay attention to.* Attention activates the information. All the thought pictures in your mind are archival–dead in a sense–until you bring them up and pay attention to them. It is essential to understand this if you are going to understand and control the mind, because it is a wonderful servant but an awful master. The mind controls most people's lives, which is a shame. It's like a donkey making a man pull the plow." He paused a moment and said, "Here, I'll show you. Do you feel particularly depressed or elated right now?"

"No, not really. Just normal, a little relaxed perhaps."

"Can I see your coffee cup?"

I handed it to him, watched him glance inside and return it, asking "Is your coffee cup half empty or half full? A simplistic question that has more to do with your phone skills than you realize. If you were to pay attention to the success and skills you already have, the blessings and miracles in your life, they will increase. Whatever you pay attention to will increase. If a baseball player who is in a batting slump goes up to the plate and mentally is paying attention to how he struck out the last three times at bat, how do you think he'll do on his fourth time at the plate?"

"Not well, that's for sure."

"Sports psychologists call it 'paralysis by analysis.' You must shift your attention from past negative experiences to the now moment which is filled with unlimited potential."

"It doesn't look so easy to me. I'm on the phone all day. I've made ten phone calls and only gotten one appointment. I begin to dread the next call. As a matter of fact I might quit for the day, at least as far as making phone calls is concerned."

"Bob, that might be a good strategy. It all depends on if it works for you. But if you only have a hammer you're going to treat everything as a nail. You could use a lot more tools, a lot more phone strategies, wouldn't you agree?"

"Yes," I answered.

"I'm curious. When you did your insurance training, didn't they tell you something like if you made one hundred phone calls per month that on the average you'd sell, let's say, four a week?"

"I don't remember the exact statistics, but yes, they had those figures."

"Well, if you found it useful, you could reframe what you call your failures, the 'no's' you get on the phone to little 'yes's.' Each 'no' you get statistically gets you closer to a 'yes.' So every 'no' is a little 'yes,' every kick is a boost. One of the characteristics of a master phoner is that they are not obsessed with perfection; they use mistakes and failures as information for self-correction, not self-flagellation.

"So how do I keep my past screw-ups from getting me down? They seem to make my self-doubt stronger."

"One way, and there are many, is to understand another aspect of the mind."

"What's that?" At this point I was ready for anything.

"That **you are not your mind**," he said, with an absolutely straight face and commanding voice.

"My mind makes me who I am, right?" I had always assumed that was true, a given. I never even questioned it.

"Wrong."

I sat in silence for a few moments. I knew the Doc was serious, but I didn't have a clue. Then I remarked, "Can you give me a hint about what you are talking about? Just a little."

He laughed till he turned red. "That was great. I loved your tone of voice when you said that." He wheeled himself over to the coffee pot and freshened our cups. As he poured, he talked, "The ancient Greeks had a triune system they called Spirit, Mind, Body. You are a spirit, immortal and powerful. At some point you entered a body. It is your vehicle. The switchboard, as it were, between you the spirit, and the body, is your mind.

"An easy way to look at it is your body's brain is the hardware, and the mind is the software. You control the body through imagery. Pictures. Holograms. Whatever you want to call it. If you want to take a sip of your coffee you first have the picture/thought and then the body follows the instruction. When you use a hammer you don't think you *are* the hammer, do you?"

"No."

"You have a car. When you get in it and drive it, you don't think you *are* a car. You know you are you driving the car, using it to get your body from one place to another. Right?"

"Right."

"So then, why would you think you are your mind? You use it. It is a useful information storage and retrieval system. It comes in real handy. But you are not it. You are the *user* of it. For example, get a picture of a tree. Got it?"

"Yup."

"You'll notice that you are the looker, the witness, the observer of the picture. You are not the picture-thought of the tree. You are simply seeing it on your screen. If you were the picture, you wouldn't be able to see it. You have to be separate from it in order to observe it."

"You're right," I said, feeling that I had just connected with something very important.

"That realization is freedom, liberation from the negative aspects of the mind. Once a person realizes they are not their pictures, thoughts or information, they have achieved liberation from the tyranny of the past."

"Well even if I know that, what happens when I'm wallowing in a negative thought or some old tape keeps running through my head and I'm stuck in it?"

"Good question. There are a lot of things you can do. You can change the color of the picture, the texture, the size, the location, the brightness, whether it's in focus, loud or soft, lots of things. Believe it or not, you can control your thoughts, your mental holograms, using this new information. Better yet, let's do something right now to change your images about the phone and your ability to excel with it."

"I'm game," I said

"All right. Let's have some fun. First, get a picture of the way you used to be with the phone. Just one picture will do, a picture that represents for you all your former negative belief systems, the actual aspects you want to change. Make it approximately 14 X 18 inches in size. About the size of a poster and make it in color."

It only took a few seconds and I had it.

"Where is the picture? Is it in front of you, upper left, lower left, upper right, or lower right?"

"It's right in front of me."

"Good. Now in the lower right hand corner of the picture put a 3 X 5 inch black-and-white holographic picture of how you *want* to be in regards to the phone."

"Black-and-white?"

"Yes."

"Even though my posture and facial expression can't be seen while on the telephone, they are an important ingredient in what I am communicating. My smile can be heard on the telephone."

"Okay, it's there."

"Wonderful. Now what we are going to do is switch those pictures when I clap my hands and say the word 'change.' You'll take the large color picture and shrink it to a 3 X 5 inch black-and-white, and at the same time take the small 3 X 5 inch black-and-white of how you want to be on the phone and blow it up to 14 X 18 inch color picture. After we've done that a few times, I'll have you do some other things with the holograms."

"I'm ready, Doc," I said playfully. And it did feel like I had known Gene Ferraro for a long time and we were old buddies playing a friendly game together.

"Okay. Have both pictures set?"

"Yup, they're both there."

"On the count of three I'll clap my hands. One, two, three, change!"

I switched the pictures, the small one expanded into a large color picture of me being a phone master, the old, negative picture shrinking almost instantly to an index card size mental picture.

"Good, now reset them back to their original sizes. We are going to repeat the procedure. You ready?"

"Yes."

"Good. One, two, three, change," he commanded with a sharp clap of his hands. The pictures switched like they did the first time only faster.

"Let's reset them again. One, two, three, change!" he repeated with a loud clap.

"Switch them again, Bob. Ready?"

"Yes."

"One, two, three!"

"Okay, they switched."

"Now reset."

"Okay."

"One, two, three, change!" And he clapped again, sending my pictures into a rapid switch.

"Now reset them Bob."

A strange thing happened all of a sudden; I couldn't reset them. "Doc, the picture of being a phone master won't change anymore. It's 14 X 18 inch color and won't reduce to 3 X 5 inch black-and-white. Is that strange?"

"No, perfect. Now take the 3 X 5 inch black-and-white of how you used to be on the phone and move that picture from in front of you to your upper left."

"Keep it the same size?"

"Yes, for the moment. Is it there?"

"Yup."

"Okay, now move it to the lower left. Now the upper right."

"Okay."

"Now put the picture on edge and spin it, just like a top when you were a kid."

"Okay, it's spinning."

"Now stop it and make the picture very gray and dim."

"Okay," I answered. The process became faster and easier each time he asked me to change the picture in some way. Something was happening, I could feel it inside my head but I had absolutely no idea what.

"Now shrink the picture to a 2 X 2 inch size."

"Done."

"Great, you're doing a good job. Now shrink it to postage stamp size."

"Okay, but I can hardly see it anymore."

"That's fine, just fine." He paused a moment and then asked, "Is it still there at the upper right of your screen?"

"Sure is."

"The world is a phone call away. I can reach people on the phone it would be impossible to reach in person."

"Good, now put it six inches in front of your face. Now six inches over your head. Then six inches behind your head. Got it?"

"Yes."

"Bring it back now to six inches in front of your face."

"It's there," I answered.

"Now put it six inches over your head again."

"Okay. It's getting easier and easier to do this."

"That's right, Bob, whether you know it or not, your mind is learning how to learn. Now put the postage-size picture behind your head again."

"Okay."

"Now one foot behind your head... five feet, ten feet, twenty feet behind your head."

"All right." I was beginning to feel very light-headed.

"Now fifty feet behind you... One hundred feet behind you."

Then suddenly it was as if some great weight had been lifted from my shoulders. But before I was even able to say anything he started talking in a high pitched, rapid-fire voice, "Now that you put that way behind you, take the picture of being a phone master, of how you want to be, and make it 2 X 4 feet in size."

By now I was really getting the hang of this. I easily expanded the picture to the larger size.

"Now make it 4 X 8 feet."

"All right."

"Now make it life size."

I nodded my head.

"You're doing great, Bob. Now turn up the color. Make it real bright."

I didn't know exactly what was going on or how this

was all working, but I could feel a big uncontrollable smile spread across my face. And the thought did pass through my head very quickly as he was talking to me—was he hypnotizing me without me even knowing it?

"That's it," he said with an enthusiastic, encouraging voice, "more color, brighter, brighter, brighter, the future is very bright." And then he abruptly stopped, leaving me floating in the most delightful, curious sensations. Parts of my body tingled. I felt completely in the moment, as if time itself had stopped.

"And now that you are so relaxed," Dr. Ferrara said in a completely different tone of voice, "I'd like to tell you a story." He rolled his wheelchair a little closer to me and began to talk to me in an odd kind of way. Almost as if he were comforting a child at bedtime. "Do you want me to close my eyes or anything?"

"No, not really. Do whatever is comfortable for you. You may laugh, or find the story boring and fall asleep, or very exciting. It doesn't matter. There is a part of you that is listening with the third ear. A very deep and special part that hears things that are not said, that makes sense of non-sense, that understands and reads the spaces between words. The empty space. And if for any reason I say or do something, verbally or non-verbally, which is not appropriate and optimum in your life, your subconscious mind will automatically change it to something more appropriate and more optimum in your life...

Once upon a time there was a very happy family with a little boy named Codey. They lived in Ohio, which as you know is a particular state in the United States. One Christmas underneath the evergreen, all decorated with bulbs and lights of different colors and shapes, were many presents all wrapped up with bows

and rainbow colored paper. Some were large and others were small.

His parents were deeply asleep upstairs still, but that didn't matter because they said he could open one present and play with it until they got up. Which one would it be? Codey picked up each one and shook it and weighed it in his little hands. He even smelled them. He showed them all to Bumper, his invisible playmate and good friend. He met Bumper one night after a bad dream. Codey's mother came into the room after hearing Codey call out and held him real close. She was so warm and soft, and kept stroking his head, and saying, 'Now, now, Codey, you don't have to be afraid of things that go bump in the night.' And the next day, after a deep and restful sleep, Bumper appeared, smiling at Codey, and chewing gum.

So Codey showed Bumper all the presents and asked him to choose. He was always right. And Bumper looked and looked and finally chose one. Well, Codey just tore off the paper in a flash of color that gave him a happy, excited feeling. That's right. And in the box was a toy telephone with two big shiny silver bells. There was a big dial with numbers and a big smiling face painted on the front of the phone. "Now," he thought to himself, "I can be just like my mom and dad, because I have my own phone and can call anybody I want in the whole wide world..."

Well, he just started right in dialing numbers and each time he put his finger into the hole and turned the dial, the bells would tingle their happy tune. He had a grand old time. He called Grandma, and Grandpa, his favorite aunt and uncle, and his friend down the street, having the most wonderful and interesting conversations until he realized that he had not even offered Bumper a chance to make a call. So he pretended that the line was busy one time and handed the phone over to Bumper who was very happy to get a chance to play with the new toy.

"Who are you going to call?"

"I'm going to call Home," Bumper replied.

"I thought this was your home, Bumper, with me, here."

"Oh, no, Codey. I just came to play with you for a while. Someday, your parents will tell you that you're too old to have an invisible playmate and I'll go back Home."

Well, as you can imagine, Codey got very sad and Bumper put his arm around him and said, "Oh, it will be okay, I'll come back someday when you most need me."

"Where are you from?" Codey asked

"I'm from a place that is invisible."

"So why can I see you?"

"Because you believe in me."

"Can I come and visit where you live sometime?"

"Sure, anytime you want."

"How about now," Codey asked.

"Sure enough, but you'll have to go back to sleep first."

"Okay, it's a deal." And Codey went back to his room with Bumper and they went to sleep. A very deep sleep during which he had the most amazing dream. Bumper was in the dream with him, as real as could be, and with a big smile on his face said out loud, "Let's go on a magical journey, Codey," and then he slowly began to float in the air.

"Can I do that too?"

"Sure. You can have many powers you are not aware of until you try something new."

"But I'm scared."

"That's okay, Codey. I was my first time, too." Bumper floated over to Codey and put his arm around him.

"I can feel your arm Bumper, it's so real. But I thought this was a dream."

'It is a dream *and* you've woken up inside the dream. Isn't it fun?"

Then Codey got out of bed and tried to float like Bumper. But he couldn't. "I can't do it Bumper," he said.

"You're just trying too hard. The more you relax the lighter you become. Just take a couple of deep breaths."

Codey started to breathe in and out slowly, and more slowly, and sure enough he began to feel lighter and lighter until, much to his own delight, he started to rise up from the floor and float in the air.

Bumper started to clap and laugh and said, "Come follow me," and they flew out the window into the early morning sky.

Higher and higher they flew far above the Earth. Codey kept giggling as if he could hardly believe what was happening. Then he noticed that the earth was crisscrossed with millions of glowing phone lines connecting every part of the world with a wonderous web of flickering lights. "The earth looks like a round Christmas tree, Bumper."

"Isn't it so pretty?"

Codey started doing fast spirals in the air, shouting with delight. Then he stopped short right next to Bumper and gave him a big hug. "You're the bestest of friends, Bumper! I'm having so much fun!"

"Me too!"

Then Codey got a very serious look on his face and asked, "What do you suppose all those people are talking about down there, Bumper? Are they all talking to their grandmas?"

Bumper laughed so hard he had to hold his tummy. "Let's say they are reaching out to touch people that live too far away to touch by hand. I like to think that all those lights down there are kisses and hugs being sent everywhere in the world all at the same time."

"I like that, but can we go home now so I don't get in trouble with Mom and Dad?"

"Don't worry, Codey. Everything's okay. Follow me, I want to show you a really neat place before we go back."

Then quicker than a flash Bumper zoomed off into the stars with Codey close behind. "Where are we going, Bumper?"

"I'm taking you to the biggest library in the whole universe!"

"Oh, what fun! Let's go faster!" And off they went. And it wasn't but a minute or two before Codey saw the brilliant blue star that Bumper seemed to be heading for.

"It's inside that star, Codey. Now hold my hand and I'll take you in."

"This is some dream," Codey thought to himself and wondered if he'd remember it when he woke up. Or forget to remember it. Then suddenly he found himself inside a magnificent and gigantic room full of books and records and computer screens and television sets and lots and lots of telephones. It was a very busy place and everyone seemed to know Bumper.

"Come over here, Codey, I want to show you something." Bumper floated over to one of the screens and typed in Codey's name.

Then the most amazing thing happened. All the pictures of Codey's life came up on the screen. "Wow, this is neat. There's Mom holding me when I was a baby. And there's me with my first wagon. That's really neat. It's like our family album at home except that it looks like a 3-D movie." As he watched, Codey saw the time when they got the phone call saying that Great-Grandpa was dead. He had cried and cried. "I feel bad," he said with tears in his eyes, "it's just like it happened now, Bumper."

"That's right. But we can change any of the pictures if you want."

"Okay, but let's just take away the hurt. Can I still have the memory of how my mom hugged me and the triple scoop ice cream cone she bought me after the funeral?"

"Sure." Bumper pushed some buttons and the pain disappeared.

"This is fun. Will I remember how to do this when I wake up at home from this dream?"

"For sure," said Bumper, "even if you need to remember to forget or forget to remember, as you get older. If you need to remember we can insert a reminder now for you to meet someone when you grow up to remind you that you have this power."

"Can we do that now, just in case?"

"Sure thing. That's my job."

"I'm your job?" Codey asked in disbelief, "I thought you were my friend."

"Oh I am, I am," Bumper said giving him a big hug. "Big Mom and Dad asked me to look out for you. I'm kind of like a guardian."

"You mean a guardian angel like they talk about in church?"

"Well, sort of," Bumper said with a laugh.

"But where are your wings?"

"My wings are my imagination."

Codey thought and thought, and then asked, "Who is Big Mom and Dad? Is that your parents?"

"They're everybody's Mom and Dad. They are the ones that created the whole universe and keep it going. They pay the electric bill for the sun and the rent for outer space."

"Neatoooooooo! I'd like to visit Big Mom and Dad right now, let's go."

"Well, we can't."

"How come," Codey asked with great disappointment. "Aren't they Home?"

"They are always Home. But it will sort of take too long to get there right now. Remember, you still have presents to open up in your life."

"Oh, yeah. I almost forgot. I'm having so much fun."

"But you can speak to them if you want. In fact, you can call them on the phone."

"Really?"

"Whenever you want, even when you are back home on earth."

"I want to call them right now. How do I do that?" Codey looked around the cosmic library for a phone, "and where's a phone we can use?"

"Oh, right," said Bumper, "follow me," and he floated over to a table and said, "Codey, we are going to imagine there is a phone on this table just like the one you have at home, okay?

"And it will just appear?"

"Absolutely."

"I'll believe it when I see it."

"Not really. When you get the hang of using your imagination you'll see it when you believe in it. Now, should we count to three?"

"That's a good idea. Ready? One. Two. Three!!!"

Pop!!—The phone with the big dial and the painted face appeared in a sudden flash of light on the table.

"Whooppee!" Codey exclaimed, "What fun!"

"Now all you have to do is dial direct to Big Mom and Dad."

"But I don't know their telephone number."

"I've got good news for you. Big Mom and Dad have an 800 number. You can dial them free of charge any time you want. Ready?"

"Oh, yes."

"Dial 8-0-0-Mom-O-Dad. See your dial, it has numbers and letters on it."

"Oh, right." Codey dialed the number and heard it ring several times and put the receiver down. "They didn't answer. How come they didn't answer?"

"Because you forgot to use your imagination."

"You're right, I did. Let's try it, I mean, let's do it again and I'll put my wings on this time." Codey dialed once more and this time Big Mom answered on the second ring.

"Hi Codey, how are you? Dad and I miss you."

"How did you know it was me, Mom?"

"Wouldn't a Mother of All know the sound of a son? I'm so glad you called. "

"Me too. Bumper showed me how."

"Isn't he just a great friend?"

"Sure is. He's really neat. Is Big Dad home?"

"He's in the Garden, trying to get rid of that snake. Do you want me to go get him?"

"That's okay. I can talk to him later. We have a garden at home, but it's winter and all covered with snow."

"Yes, I know, and you help your parents with the weeding."

"I sure do," Codey said proudly.

"I just want you to know that you are a very special person and we love you very very much. Remember to treat people the way you would like to be treated and everything will be okay. Say hello to your parents for me and remember to give us a call often ,and let us know how things are going, or if you need anything."

"I promise."

"A big kiss and hug to you. I better go now and finish dinner. Talk to you soon. Bye."

"Bye."

...in the next hours, days, weeks, and months ahead you will find yourself feeling more and more loving, patient, forgiving of yourself and others, more focused and powerful, especially while using the telephone, that without knowing exactly how you did it, you love yourself more and trust yourself more. . . . One. Two. Three. Eyes open.

I guess I must have fallen to sleep while Dr. Ferrara was telling me the story. When my eyes opened I was a little groggy at first and then a few minutes later I felt refreshed and rejuvenated, as if I had slept hours and hours. When I looked at my watch only fifteen minutes had gone by. He looked at me with a smile and took a tape out of his recorder and handed it to me, "Play this story a couple of times per week for a month Bob, and I think you are going to be delightfully surprised at the results."

"Whatever you say Doc. Sorry I fell asleep on you. I'm kind of embarrassed."

"Actually," he said with a laugh, "it's a compliment."

* * *

O'RYAN'S PHONEMASTERY NOTES:

1) Whatever thoughts and mental image pictures you hold in your mind affect you, even down to the cellular layer. Your self-image, who you think and define yourself as being, dramatically influences your body shape, health, habits, personal relationships, prosperity level, spiritual level and especially your phone skills.

2) There is no such thing as hypnosis. There is only a very special and effective kind of communication both with one's own self and others.

3) **Personal growth is a process, not a product.**

4) "Trance" is a natural state like daydreaming. The mind produces alpha and theta brainwaves which characterize the trance state. This state is achieved naturally during different times during the day and night and consciously by relaxing the body and thinking of a pleasant experience or place. There are many different names for this: visualizations, guided imagery, progressive relaxation, autogenic training, self-hypnosis, meditation, daydreaming and in some cases, praying.

5) The mind is likened to a bio-computer and acts as an information, storage and retrieval system. We take mental holograms (three-dimensional pictures made with laser light) of everything that happens to us during our lives—what we see, hear, taste, smell and feel. When we recall the "mental pictures," we are using our memory.

6) All mental images, holographic thought-pictures, are past information, archival in nature, and do not necessarily have anything to do with the present.

7) Attention is the key to activating the information stored in the memory bank of holograms. If we pay attention to a depressing memory, we will begin to feel depressed even though it is not happening "now." The same with happy or empowering memories. **Whatever you pay attention to increases.**

8) You are not any of your thoughts or memories, you are a spirit, inhabiting a body and are the viewer of stored data, the observer, the witness, the photographer. You are not the pictures. You are the one who is in control of which thoughts or belief systems to pay attention to and activate.

9) There are many ways to control these mental holograms, even if you are not consciously aware of it. Consciously you can change their color, size, location, the brightness, the focus, the volume of the sound, or the speed of the "movie" of the event.

10) **Each of us has a "higher self" or guardian** which is a powerful resource and guide. We may have forgotten that.

11) Big Mom & Dad of the Universe have an 800 number and everyone can dial direct. If anyone tells you they are the only one who is in possession of God's unlisted number, they are not telling the truth.

MAY THE CIRCUITS
BE UNBROKEN

It's funny how easy it is to forget that things were not always the way they are right now.

Yesterday I was sitting in my new office, with my computer in front of me. I had my new headset phone on, which I had gotten so I could leave both hands free to type notes to myself on the computer during my frequent phone conversations.

Aside from winning my company's annual award for bringing in the most new customers, I found that my newly acquired confidence on the phone had carried over to many other areas of my life, even at home. I felt more comfortable with myself, I liked myself more, I liked my job, I developed a lot more friendships with the people at my office. It was an incredible transformation, and all within nine months.

In between calls I often practiced the self-hypnosis/relaxation techniques I learned from Dr. Ferrara, visualizing the next task I had to perform, or the next completed transaction. Acquiring my new corner office with the window overlooking the park was a result of one of my visualizations. My intercom buzzed, interrupting my reverie. "Mr. Ryan," my secretary's voice began, "your conference call is ready. I have Mr. Partridge in Los Angeles and his wife in Honolulu on the line."

As always, hearing Donna's melodious voice was a pleasure. I remembered interviewing dozens of applicants for the job of my assistant. The heart of my interview was to ask each applicant what they thought was the essence of phone excellence. Without hesitation Donna had looked me straight in the eye and gave me a one word answer, "kindness."

I hired her on the spot.

Coming back to present time, I said, "Thank you, Donna. Please put them through."

Mr. and Mrs. Partridge both began speaking at once. I laughed inside at how this would have thrown the old me. After timing the rhythm of their speech patterns and tuning in to their breathing rates I began to conduct a sweet three-part harmony. The policy questions they had were quickly settled, and the call was over before I really got warmed up.

My intercom buzzed again. "Yes, Donna?"

"Mr. Ryan, there's a Walter Rensin waiting for you in the outer office. Should I send him in?"

This was the man who had called yesterday, and mumbled so badly into the phone I almost couldn't make out what he was saying. He finally managed to say that JD had suggested he make an appointment with me. My life had gotten so full I hadn't spoken with JD in a couple of months. I wondered if this Rensin fellow was an insurance referral.

"Okay, send him in."

Walter Rensin entered, looking warily about the office. He wasn't bad-looking, but he had a stooped posture, low voice, and wrinkled clothes. Walter gave the general impression of low self-esteem.

I stood and offered my hand. "Hello Walter, glad to meet you. I understand you know JD?"

Walter's handshake was as weak as his appearance. His eyes looked down at the top of my desk as we spoke.

"Yes. I met him in an airport a couple of days ago. We were both stranded for a few hours while they rescheduled our flight. I was having a terrible time because it meant that I had to change some appointments and I had to call my people and tell them."

"What's so terrible about that?"

"Well, you see, I'm terrified of the phone. In fact, that's why I'm here. JD said you had some secrets for becoming more skilled at using the phone. And he seemed to think you wouldn't mind letting me in on some of them."

That sly fox! I turned to look out the window so Walter Rensin wouldn't misinterpret the wide grin on my face. I didn't want him to think I was laughing at him. As I turned back to him, I reached into my top drawer and pulled out a summary of all my Phonemaster Notes. I handed it to Walter and said, "Secrets? Well, I must admit, I do have a few secrets."

* * *

THE DOZEN DO'S OF PHONE EXCELLENCE

1. Remember you have magic at your fingertips. You can instantly talk to anyone—you have the whole word in your hands.

2. Listen unto others as you would have others listen unto you.

3. What you say is far less important than how you say it.

4. Establish rapport by speaking the same language as the other person. People perceive the world, and express themselves through seeing, hearing, and feeling.

5. Act as if you have all the time in the world for each call.

6. Consider sacred the other person's feelings and view of the universe. True kindness comes from understanding that it's real for them.

7. Remind yourself to breathe and relax.

8. Be patient. Learning new phone skills is dependent on pretending that you already have them.

9. Remember LAF: Love, Appropriateness and Flexibility.

10. De-fuzz your conversations by asking the clarifying questions of who, what, where, when, why, and how.

11. God has an 800 number and everyone can dial direct.

12. You already knew all this. Be natural and trust yourself.

ABOUT THE AUTHORS

PETER BLUM spent over 20 years in the field of communication, working in publishing, bookstores, and as a journalist and editor for newspapers, magazines, and medical periodicals. He has also been involved since the early 1970s in the study and practice of various meditation and spiritual techniques and philosophies. After initial training in Futureshaping from Richard A. Zarro, he studied with the New York Training Institute for NLP, the National Guild of Hypnotists (NGH), and Whole Brain Functioning (WBF). He is currently a Certified Instructor of Basic and Advanced Clinical Hypnosis for the NGH and a Trainer for WBF. He has a private practice in Woodstock and New York City, and for the past several years has been in charge of the Stress Management Department of the Rhinebeck Health Center. He has given corporate trainings and personal growth workshops at the Phoenicia Pathwork, the Open Spoke Ranch, and the Omega Institute for Holistic Studies, and has been a frequent guest lecturer at the New Age Health Spa.

RICHARD A. ZARRO is the founder and president of Futureshaping Technologies, Inc., a company which presents seminars to individuals and businesses around the world. His expertise in the techniques of communications excellence, telephone skills, and peak performance states has made him a much sought after speaker and seminar leader. Having implemented Mr. Zarro's techniques, corporations, sales professionals, and business executives report powerful and lasting results. In addition, clients from around the world visit Mr. Zarro for private consultation.

Known for his humor, passion, and distinct approach to critical business topics, Mr. Zarro has been invited to train executives for such corporate giants as IBM, Panasonic, MetLife, Alco Standard, and others.

Mr. Zarro is also a highly acknowledged pioneer and leader in the field of hypnosis. His work has been quoted in mainstream publications and bestselling books. In 1990, he became an International Hypnosis Hall of Fame Inductee. In 1994, his work in metaphysics was honored with the distinguished "Unlimited Spirit Award" by the International Association of Counselors and Therapists (IACT). Certified by the Society of NeuroLinguistic Programming, Mr. Zarro has done extensive training with NLP's co-developer, the internationally acclaimed linguist Dr. John Grinder. Because of his ability to speak on so many topics of public interest, Mr. Zarro is a frequent guest on radio and television shows.

As a private consultant, public speaker and author, Mr. Zarro is committed to bringing the cutting-edge tools of NLP and Futureshaping Technologies to the world.

Mr. Zarro is the co-author of *Changing Your Destiny* (Metamorphous Press) and the creator of many self-empowerment, peak performance, and communications excellence tapes. For more information on products, seminars and consultations, call (914) 679-7655.

For more information . . .

FUTURESHAPING TECHNOLOGIES, INC., is an organization that believes that the business community—because it already has a multinational, global perspective—is in a unique position to spearhead the transformation of global markets. FTI delivers perspectives and techniques coming out of the latest research at major universities. It is dedicated to facilitating the business world's ability to provide peace and growth through prosperity and harmony. Communication is the thread from which the fabric of business is woven. Successful business executives understand how to effectively and efficiently influence others in the directions of growth. The successful secrets of these individuals are now available to be easily modeled and learned. After years of research, FTI has designed a series of seminars and products which give an individual the highly defined skills that quality communication requires.

If you are interested in further training for yourself or your business, write FTI, P.O. Box 489, Woodstock, New York 12948, or call (914) 679-7655. Richard Zarro and Peter Blum, authors of *The PhoneBook,* are available through FTI for consultation or seminars in telephone skills and strategies, as well as seminars and keynote speeches in:

- stress management
- communication excellence
- peak performance in sales
- The New Passion: Futureshaping Business In The Time Of Global Transition

and personal consultations in:
- motivation
- conflict resolution
- goal setting
- personal empowerment

FTI also offers audio and video training cassettes, other training products, and a free newsletter listing dates and locations of FTI presentations.

METAMORPHOUS PRESS

Metamorphous Press is a publisher of books and other media providing resources for personal growth and positive change. MP publishes leading-edge ideas that help people strengthen their unique talents and discover that they are responsible for their own realities. Many of our titles center around Neurolinguistic Programming (NLP). NLP is an exciting, practical, and powerful model of observable patterns of behavior and communication and the processes that underlie them.

Metamorphous Press provides selections in many useful subject areas such as communication, health and fitness, education, business and sales, therapy, selections for young persons, and other subjects of general and specific interest. Our products are available in fine bookstores around the world.

Our distributors for North America are:

Baker & Taylor
Bookpeople
Ingram
Inland Book Co.
Metamorphous
    Advanced Product Services

Moving Books, Inc.
New Leaf
Pacific Pipeline
The Distributors

For those of you overseas, we are distributed by:

Airlift (UK, Western Europe)
Specialist Publications (Australia)

New selections are added regularly and availability and prices change, so ask for a current catalog or to be put on our mailing list. If you have difficulty finding our products in your favorite store, or if you prefer to order by mail, we will be happy to make our books and other products available to you directly. Your involvement and interest in what we do is always welcome. Please write or call us at:

Metamorphous Press
P.O. Box 10616
Portland, OR 97210
TEL (503) 228-4972
FAX (503) 223-9117

TOLL FREE ORDERING
1-800-937-7771

Related Titles Available From
Metamorphous Press

If you are unable to obtain *The Phone Book* at your favorite bookstore, you are welcome to order directly from us by one of the following:

- **Call toll free with your credit card number**
  1-800-937-7771
- **Mail this form with your credit card number**
- **Mail this form, including $10.95 check or money order for each copy.**
  Shipping—first copy: add $3.95
  Each additional copy: add $1.00

VISA_____ MC_____ AMEX_____ OPTIMA_____

Day Phone_____

Card Number _____

Expiration Date_____

Signature_____

Billing Address (☐ Residence ☐ Commercial)

_____

_____

_____

Orders sent UPS to street addresses (7-10 days), bookrate to P.O. Boxes (2-4 weeks).

	Quantity	Total
The Phone Book	_____ x $10.95 ea.	_____
Shipping/Handling		_____
TOTAL		_____

Cut on the dotted line and mail (or fax) to: Metamorphous Press, P.O. Box 10616, Portland, OR 97210-0616. Thank you!

‑ ‑

Fold here

Place
stamp
here

Metamorphous Press
P.O. Box 10616
Portland, OR 97210-0616